KNOWING ME, KNOWING YOU

KNOWING ME, KNOWING YOU

strategies for sex education in the primary school

Pete Sanders and Liz Swinden

Illustrated by
Pat Murray and Cecilia Fitzsimons

Note to the teacher:
Each worksheet in this book has been
marked to indicate whether it is intended for teacher (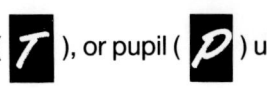), or pupil (𝒫) use.

The authors would like to thank Steve Myers for his help and
support with this book.

Knowing me, knowing you
LD949
ISBN 1 85503 071 3
© Pete Sanders, Liz Swinden
© illustrations Pat Murray
© anatomical drawings Cecilia Fitzsimons
All rights reserved
First published 1990

LDA, Duke Street, Wisbech, Cambs, PE13 2AE

Contents

1

Everything you ever wanted to know about sex education...

☐ What is Sex Education?

If sex education were merely about biological functions, then our job as teachers would be simply to pass on certain biological information about the way in which our bodies operate. We all know, however, that this is not the case. The HMI Document, *Health Education 5 – 16* Curriculum Matters No. 6, 1986, HMSO, states that:

> In sex education, factual information about the physical aspects of sex, though important, is not more important than consideration of the qualities of the values, standards and the exercise of personal responsibility as they affect individuals and the community at large.
>
> Para 44, p. 17

According to this view, sex education is about helping children to make responsible decisions about the relationships that they form with others. When considering ourselves in relation to others, the area of self-esteem also comes into play. Helping children to develop a positive sense of self will involve discussion about choice-making, assertiveness, self-expression and, in turn, respect for others.

Values and Attitudes

To teach sex education according to such a view obviously presents us with a far greater teaching challenge. For one thing, it will be impossible to teach sex education in a meaningful way without having our own values, attitudes and taboos challenged. We must recognise that these have been formed by such factors as our age, class, sex and sexuality, as well as the culture with which we identify. Then there is the variety or lack of experiences that we have had ourselves. To some, sex may be embarrassing or a mystery. Some may fear that they are not in sympathy with societal values or those of their colleagues. Many worry about the use of appropriate and inappropriate language.

No teacher wants to put a child into a state of value confusion, but what if we present a 'norm' that is vastly at odds with that of the child's home, religion or culture? Extending children's perspectives in terms of the wider world, while at the same time respecting the values of their own world, is indeed a delicate and difficult task.

Some would suggest that these are questions which we do not need to worry about. Primary school children are too young for sex education; that should be left to the secondary teachers. Others would argue that the responsibility lies with the parents and not with teachers anyway! However, research carried out between 1982 and 1986 by the Guttmacher Institute indicated clearly that the lowest teenage pregnancy rates were found in countries where, along with other factors, there were effective programmes of sex education. (*Pregnancy, Conception and Family Planning Services in Industrialised Countries*, Yale University Press, 1989.)

3

Without a doubt, primary-aged children are exposed to many different messages in the media about sex and sexuality, long before they enter secondary school. Clearly, pupils need help in learning how to process these different messages which are powerfully conveyed to them every day.

However anxious teachers may be to hand back the responsibility into the laps of parents, research indicates that parents would much prefer that sex education take place in schools rather than at home. Isobel Allen's (1987) study, *Education in Sex and Personal Relationships*, showed that 96 per cent of parents questioned wanted their child's school to take the responsibility.

Some schools, whilst accepting the responsibility for sex education, involve outside agencies. They may ask a health visitor or a school nurse to deliver one-off sessions. This approach has severe shortcomings, however, since the whole area of personal relationships is not a 'bolted-on' part of learning. People *relate* across the curriculum, in both formal and informal settings. It is one of the greatest assets of being human. Failure to encourage children to learn and understand this is to deprive them of an essential part of existence.

So, whether we like it or not, there is a need for sex education in the primary school. There is a call for it from parents and the responsibility lies with the teacher and the school.

☐ Sex education and the law

Until the 1986 Education Act produced a new framework within which all teachers in state schools now have to operate, there was virtually no guidance at all about sex education. Schools were free to include it in the curriculum or not, and teachers could decide for themselves the content of sex education and the teaching methods and resources that they used.

See if you can answer the following questions about the changes which the 1986 Act has brought about. The answers are at the end of the section.

___ Are the following statements true or false? ___

1 School governors have a responsibility for determining policy on both the content and organisation of sex education within the school. ☐T☐ ☐F☐

2 Governors do not have to listen to the views of the headteacher, staff or anyone connected with the community served by the school. ☐T☐ ☐F☐

3 Homosexuality must not be included in sex education. ☐T☐ ☐F☐

4   Schools should be prepared to teach about contraception and
abortion.   ☐T ☐F

5   School governors need training about sex education.   ☐T ☐F

6   Schools catering for children with special educational needs are
exempt from the law regarding sex education.   ☐T ☐F

7   Parents have a statutory right to withdraw their children from sex
education lessons.   ☐T ☐F

8   Governors must consult with the local Chief Officer of Police over
their sex education policy.   ☐T ☐F

9   Teachers may make use of the expertise of Health Service
professionals in implementing sex education policy at classroom
level.   ☐T ☐F

10 Teachers and other education service professionals need to be fully
informed about HIV/AIDS.   ☐T ☐F

It is clear from this that teachers need to be in possession of
up-to-date, accurate information about the legal implications of sex
education. Although this will chiefly apply to secondary schools, it
would be foolish for primary schools to ignore the area. Children
will always ask questions; who are we to deny them the best
answers available?

The main examples of recent legislation with which teachers should
be familiar are as follows.

- *Education (School Information) Regulations 1981*   These require
  LEAs to publish particulars of their schools' curricula. The
  particulars must contain information about 'the manner and content
  in which education as respects sexual matters is given.'

- *Education Act (No 2) 1986*   This gave school governing bodies the
  responsibility for deciding whether or not sex education should
  form part of the curriculum and for making a policy regarding its
  content and organisation. The Act also refers to sex education being
  'given in such a manner as to encourage pupils to have due regard to
  moral considerations and the value of family life'.

  We would hope that the passing of this Act does not mean that the
  good work done in this area by many primary schools in the past
  will stop as a result of the decisions of some governing bodies.

- *DES Circular 11/87 'Sex Education at school'*   This looks in more
  detail at a variety of topics including the role of governors,
  headteachers, parents, etc.

- *Gillick* v.*DHSS*   You may recall that in 1985 Mrs Victoria Gillick brought a case against the DHSS, seeking to:

  > try to establish that it was unlawful to give young persons under the age of 16 contraceptive advice and/or treatment without their parents' consent. The House of Lords ruled against her.
  >
  > *Sexual issues, the law and the teacher's responsibility*, Assistant Masters and Mistresses Association, 1987

  Although teachers in primary schools are working with children who, with very few exceptions, are not sexually active and capable of reproducing, they should be aware of the ruling which came out of the case, since it caused a great deal of confusion about what teachers could or could not say to pupils. The AMMA booklet explains the matter thus:

  > The Gillick case makes clear that a teacher does not act unlawfully in giving information about contraception without parental consent – although s/he should act within the terms of the school's sex education policy.

- *Clause 28*   This concerns the 'promotion' of homosexuality. As with the Gillick case, Section 28 of the Local Government Bill, which was passed in 1988, caused much controversy whilst it was being debated. Inevitably it gave many people, including teachers, the idea that it was going to be illegal to talk about homosexuality in schools. This idea is erroneous.

  Whilst the law does say that local authorities may not support anything which 'promotes or encourages' homosexuality, this does *not* apply to sex education in the school curriculum. This means that teachers may give information and allow discussion about it. Although this will be more appropriate to the secondary school situation, teachers of much younger pupils know that it is a topic that pre-pubertal children often want to question and talk about.

  It is an area where there is still a considerable amount of myth and misunderstanding. (When the government AIDS campaign started, primary school playgrounds abounded with rhymes and songs about it.) This was at a time when the tabloid press was linking it with certain so-called 'at risk groups' rather than 'risky' behaviour. It is therefore a subject that needs to be fully discussed by staff, parents and governors. We cannot allow situations where the prejudices of adults are passed on, unchallenged, to the next generation.

Answers to the quiz

1   TRUE. Refer to Sections 8 and 9 of the DES Circular No. 11/87, *Sex Education at school.*

2   FALSE. Section 6 of the DES Circular states that 'governors will be required under the Act to have regard to any representations made

to them by any persons connected with the community served by the school… The Secretary of State expects that governors will find useful the professional advice which the head and other staff are able to offer.' However, the final decision on sex education rests with the governors.

3   FALSE. The Circular states that 'there is no place in any school in any circumstances for any teaching which advocates homosexual behaviour, which presents it as the "norm" or which encourages homosexual experimentation by pupils' (Section 22). This does not mean that the subject cannot be discussed or mentioned.

4   TRUE. Section 21 of the Circular acknowledges that pupils are bound to ask questions and that 'schools should be prepared to offer balanced and factual information and to acknowledge the major ethical issues'.

5   TRUE. The DES Circular does not address itself to the issue of training for governors. However, given that school governors come from a wide variety of backgrounds and often have no particular knowledge of the subject, let alone expertise, it would be foolish to ignore their needs. Many LEAs are now offering training to their governing bodies on a variety of subjects, and the Health Education Authority will shortly be publishing materials on this aspect of governor training. On p. 31 of this book there is a workshop which looks at how governors can be enabled to consider various aspects of sex education and their responsibility for it.

6   FALSE. The 11/87 Circular states that 'special schools have a particularly sensitive role to play. . . . Children with learning difficulties need more help than others in coping with the physical and emotional aspects of growing up. . . . Governors of special schools . . . will need to take particular care in working out their policy.'

7   FALSE. Circular 11/87 states that governors 'have the discretion to accept or reject requests from parents for their children to be withdrawn from any Sex Education to which they object', but there is no statutory right. Governors are urged to acknowledge that some parents will have strong objections on religious grounds, and to bear this in mind when exercising their discretion.

8   FALSE. However, governors must 'have regard to any representations made to them by any persons connected with the community served by the school, and to any representations made by the Chief Officer of Police connected with his responsibilities'.

9   TRUE.

10 TRUE. In order to help with this, the DES issued a factual booklet, *AIDS: Some Questions and Answers* (1987). There is also a wide range of other materials, both for use with pupils and for teacher reference. See the resources section in Chapter 7 of this book.

☐ **This book's approach to sex education**

Bearing in mind the sizeable responsibility and challenge that sex education carries, we clearly need to give as much consideration to the *way* in which we teach as to *what* we teach. For example, it is very difficult to develop self-esteem in children by merely giving a lecture about it.

The workshop approach that is adopted in this book offers teachers carefully structured, practical ideas which in turn will afford children access to experiential learning in a cross-curricular setting.

The book sets out to provide practical ways in which to help children to understand how bodies work and how they change, and to assist them to understand their own attitudes and values and those of others. The activities are designed to help children to understand their own physical, emotional and social development within the context both of those around them and of society at large with all its cultural variations. The workshops are also designed to assist the teacher in disseminating factual information and correcting any misunderstandings that the children may have. A guide to the contents of each activity starts on p. 10.

Whilst we recognise that individual teachers will prefer one particular style of learning, we hope that the workshop approach will offer reassurance to children and will encourage them to explore choices within the classroom environment (particularly since so many decisions which concern them outside the classroom are made for them).

Throughout the book, our aim is to encourage children actively to analyse their own role in developing positive, responsible and caring attitudes. This involves offering them the opportunity to explore and reflect on all kinds of ideas in a non-threatening way which is carefully structured to be accepting and non-judgemental.

A whole school policy

Having recognised the worries that are created by teaching sex education, it is important to address them. Working together as a whole staff is highly appropriate here. By exploring adult values together with colleagues, it is possible to reach a consensus about appropriate learning across the whole school. To assist in this process, ideas for workshops with teachers, parents and governors are included in this book (see pp. 31–40).

An initial brainstorming session on 'What is sex education?' will very likely generate a list similar to this:

Self-reflection

Sense of self

Respect

Values

Self-respect and confidence

Knowing how our bodies work

Appropriate ways of expressing feelings

Information

Gender stereotyping

Sexually transmitted diseases (STDs)

Activity

Affection

Relationships

Birth and reproduction

Families

Growth and change

Communication

Responsibility

Contraception

Power

Peer group pressure

Pleasure / pain

What influences our behaviour

Friendship

Legislation

De-mystifying the myths

Choices

Assertion

Causes and effects of behaviour

☐ **Guide to the activities**

Title	*Dealing with*	*Relating to*
Chapter 2		
1 Brainstorming our aims	Identifying and prioritising aims.	Teaching methodology
2 Growing into group work	Identifying appropriate ways of working with children.	Teaching methodology
3 Chalk and talk	Identifying appropriate ways of working with children.	Teaching methodology
4 Teacher skills	Identification of teacher skills.	Teaching methodology 7 *ABC of children's skills*
5 Role review	Approaches to group work.	Teaching methodology
6 Language and sex	Analysing adult feelings about words used to describe sexual organs and sexual activities.	Adult attitudes
7 ABC of children's skills	Identification of skills which are developed through using the activities in this book.	4 *Teacher skills*
8 Sex education workshop	Awareness of the breadth of sex education and identification of what children need to know.	1 *Brainstorming our aims* 2 *Growing into group work* 3 *Chalk and talk* 4 *Teacher skills* 5 *Role review* 6 *Language and sex*
9 Human bingo	Encourage group participants to get to know each other.	Effective group work
Chapter 3		
10 ABC of workshop ideas	Activities to promote co-operative learning.	Most of the teaching ideas in the book
11 How was it for you?	Evaluation activities to encourage children to reflect and comment on what they have learned and done.	Children's attitudes
12 The 'Visitor experience'	Ways to engage children in planning and receiving visitors to their classroom.	Teaching styles

Title	Dealing with	Relating to
Chapter 4		
13 Who am I?	Developing self-awareness and confidence.	14 *ABC of personal qualities* 15 *My personal coat of arms* 16 *A collage of me* 17 *Different parts of me* 22 *What I need/What I want* 23 *Graphing out our needs and wants* 24 *My ideal day*
14 ABC of personal qualities	Celebrating personal qualities.	13 *Who am I?* 15 *My personal coat of arms* 17 *Different parts of me* 19 *Qualities I look for in people* 20 *Personal tags*
15 My personal coat of arms	Celebrating personal qualities.	13 *Who am I?* 14 *ABC of personal qualities* 16 *A collage of me*
16 A collage of me	Enhancing a sense of self-identity.	13 *Who am I?* 15 *My personal coat of arms*
17 Different parts of me	How we are perceived by other people.	13 *Who am I?* 14 *ABC of personal qualities* 20 *Personal tags*
18 We're all different	Physical differences between people.	Work concerning parts of the body
19 Qualities I look for in people	Analysing personal perceptions of qualities.	14 *ABC of personal qualities*
20 Personal tags	Developing respect for others.	14 *ABC of personal qualities* 17 *Different parts of me*
21 Plotting people	Analysing how people relate to each other.	31 *Risk factor* 32 *How I keep myself safe* 33 *Who can I turn to?* 36 *Boys and girls go out to play* 52 *Forces of persuasion*
22 What I need /What I want	Similarities and differences.	13 *Who am I?* 23 *Graphing out our needs and wants* 24 *My ideal day*
23 Graphing out our needs and wants	Differentiating between needs and wants.	13 *Who am I?* 22 *What I need/What I want* 24 *My ideal day*

Title	Dealing with	Relating to
24 My ideal day	Identifying personal needs and wants.	13 *Who am I?* 22 *What I need/What I want* 23 *Graphing out our needs and wants*
25 Bar chart feelings graph	Expression of feelings.	26 *Feeling barometers* 27 *My personal feelings log* 28 *Painting a feeling* 29 *The feelings collection* 30 *Circles of feelings*
26 Feeling barometers	Expression of feelings.	25 *Bar chart feelings graph* 27 *My personal feelings log* 28 *Painting a feeling* 29 *The feelings collection* 30 *Circles of feelings*
27 My personal feelings log	Analysing personal reactions to situations.	25 *Bar chart feelings graph* 26 *Feeling barometers* 28 *Painting a feeling* 29 *The feelings collection* 30 *Circles of feelings*
28 Painting a feeling	Expressions of feelings and differences/similarities.	25 *Bar chart feelings graph* 26 *Feeling barometers* 27 *My personal feelings log* 29 *The feelings collection* 30 *Circles of feelings*
29 The feelings collection	Identifying positive and negative feelings.	25 *Bar chart feelings graph* 26 *Feeling barometers* 27 *My personal feelings log* 28 *Painting a feeling* 30 *Circles of feelings* 61 *Attraction reaction* 62 *Reading our feelings*
30 Circles of feelings	Phrases used to express feelings.	25 *Bar chart feelings graph* 26 *Feeling barometers* 27 *My personal feelings log* 28 *Painting a feeling* 29 *The feelings collection*
31 Risk factor	Identifying risks and strategies for handling them.	21 *Plotting people* 32 *How I keep myself safe* 52 *Forces of persuasion*
32 How I keep myself safe	Personal safety.	21 *Plotting people* 31 *Risk factor* 52 *Forces of persuasion*

Title	Dealing with	Relating to
33 Who can I turn to?	Identifying significant people that children can trust.	21 *Plotting people*
34 I enjoy being . . .	Stereotyping.	35 *ABC of jobs* 37 *Sherlock Holmes* 38 *Picture triggers*
35 ABC of jobs	Stereotyping.	34 *I enjoy being . . .* 37 *Sherlock Holmes* 38 *Picture triggers*
36 Boys and girls go out to play	Gender issues in the playground.	21 *Plotting people*
37 Sherlock Holmes	Stereotyping.	34 *I enjoy being . . .* 35 *ABC of jobs* 38 *Picture triggers*
38 Picture triggers	Stereotyping.	31 *Risk factor* 34 *I enjoy being . . .* 35 *ABC of jobs* 37 *Sherlock Holmes*

Chapter 5

Title	Dealing with	Relating to
39 Words, words, words	Identifying ways that we use language.	58 *Suggestion box* 59 *Questions in a hat*
40 I can understand you	Familiarising children with medical words and their pronunciation.	Any new words which are introduced to the children
41 Body talk	Identifying body parts and discussing personal safety.	42 *Naming the frame* 43 *Fishing for facts* 45 *Female or male?* 52 *Forces of persuasion* 63 *Checking out the facts*
42 Naming the frame	Identifying body parts and children's attitudes to them.	41 *Body talk* 43 *Fishing for facts* 45 *Female or male?* 58 *Suggestion box* 59 *Questions in a hat* 63 *Checking out the facts*
43 Fishing for facts	Identifying body parts.	41 *Body talk* 42 *Naming the frame* 44 *Getting organised* 45 *Female or male?* 63 *Checking out the facts*

Title	Dealing with	Relating to
44 Getting organised	Identifying internal organs.	43 *Fishing for facts* 45 *Female or male?* 63 *Checking out the facts*
45 Female or male?	Identification of body parts and which gender they apply to.	41 *Body talk* 42 *Naming the frame* 43 *Fishing for facts* 44 *Getting organised* 63 *Checking out the facts*
46 Guess the baby	Growth and change.	47 *A day in the life* 48 *Retrographs* 51 *Good time lines* 53 *Puberty quiz* 54 *Puberty!*
47 A day in the life	Growth, change and responsibilities.	46 *Guess the baby* 48 *Retrographs*
48 Retrographs	Growth, change and responsibilities.	46 *Guess the baby* 47 *A day in the life* 49 *Tracking time* 51 *Good time lines* 53 *Puberty quiz* 54 *Puberty!*
49 Tracking time	Personal history.	46 *Guess the baby* 48 *Retrographs* 50 *Family favourites* 51 *Good time lines*
50 Family favourites	Celebration of group events.	49 *Tracking time* 51 *Good time lines*
51 Good time lines	Celebrating life events.	46 *Guess the baby* 48 *Retrographs* 49 *Tracking time* 50 *Family favourites*
52 Forces of persuasion	Identifying personal responsibilities and peer-group pressure.	21 *Plotting people* 31 *Risk factor* 32 *How I keep myself safe* 41 *Body talk*
53 Puberty quiz	Assessing children's knowledge of puberty.	46 *Guess the baby* 48 *Retrographs* 54 *Puberty!*
54 Puberty!	Understanding changes during puberty.	46 *Guess the baby* 48 *Retrographs* 53 *Puberty quiz*

Title	Dealing with	Relating to
55 What is menstru-ation?	Informing children about menstruation.	53 *Puberty quiz* 54 *Puberty!* 56 *Why wash?* 57 *Kim's game*
56 Why wash?	Personal hygiene and its cost.	55 *What is menstruation?* 57 *Kim's game*
57 Kim's game	Hygiene.	55 *What is menstruation?* 56 *Why wash?*

Chapter 6

Title	Dealing with	Relating to
58 Suggestion box	Enabling children to ask questions in a non-threatening way.	59 *Questions in a hat*
59 Questions in a hat	Enabling children to express concerns in a non-threatening way.	58 *Suggestion box*
60 Videowatch	Identifying areas of knowledge before and after using a video resource.	List of resources
61 Attraction reaction	Analysing how people express attraction.	29 *The feelings collection* 62 *Reading our feelings*
62 Reading our feelings	Identifying how people express their feelings.	29 *The feelings collection* 61 *Attraction reaction*
63 Checking out the facts	Knowledge about sexual activity and reproduction.	41 *Body talk* 42 *Naming the frame* 43 *Fishing for facts* 44 *Getting organised* 45 *Female or male?* 69 *Know-how*
64 Circle round the truth	Assessing children's understanding of sexual activity.	Any work on sexual activity
65 What is mastur-bation?	Clarifying questions which children may have about masturbation.	Any work on sexual activity 72–76 *Continuum activities*
66 Happy birthways!	Different methods of birth.	67 *Link the baby with its carer* 68 *Stages of pregnancy* 69 *Know-how*
67 Link the baby with its carer	Names of animals and their young, and different methods of birth.	66 *Happy birthways!* 68 *Stages of pregnancy* 69 *Know-how*

Title	*Dealing with*	*Relating to*
68 Stages of pregnancy	How a baby grows inside the body.	66 *Happy birthways!* 67 *Link the baby with its carer* 69 *Know-how*
69 Know-how	Knowledge about reproduction.	63 *Checking out the facts* 66 *Happy birthways!* 67 *Link the baby with its carer* 68 *Stages of pregnancy*
70 Barriers	The concept of contraception.	71 *Baby talk*
71 Baby talk	Arguments for and against having children.	70 *Barriers*
72 Whole class continuum A: facts	Areas of knowledge.	Any area where knowledge needs to be explored
73 Small group continuum A: facts	Areas of knowledge.	Any area where knowledge needs to be explored
74 Whole class continuum B: feelings	Exploring issues.	Any area where attitudes, values, issues need to be explored
75 Small group continuum B: feelings	Exploring issues.	Any area where attitudes, values, issues need to be explored
76 Continuum activities: suggested statements	Suggested statements.	Any area where attitudes, values, issues need to be explored
77 Diamond fours/nines	Exploring issues.	Any area where issues are being discussed
78 Diamond fours/nines: suggested statements	Suggested statements.	Any area where issues are being discussed
79 *Aide-mémoire*	Helping teachers to remember areas which they may wish to include in their teaching programme.	1 *Brainstorming our aims* 4 *Teacher skills* 6 *Language and sex* 8 *Sex education workshop*

Chapter 7

80 Resources workshop	To generate criteria for selection of sex education resources.	Any area where resources are being assessed

·2·

It is what you do and the way that you do it

☐ Teaching styles

Although we may be well aware that everyone learns in different ways and that no one teaching style is the panacea, research shows that most of us tend to teach in the way that we ourselves were taught. We may consider that a didactic approach is appropriate for some learning. However, the 'chalk and talk' method can lead to conformity and often does not require the learner to show initiative and individual thought. It can mean that knowledge is transmitted efficiently and this may be seen as an advantage with large groups.

Certainly, by using didactic methods we can ensure that our aims are monitored easily. But if this is the only teaching style that we employ, we are at risk of helping only a certain number of children. Others may not be motivated by this approach and may feel that they have failed if they are not able to recall ideas easily or are not ready to handle a particular concept. Perhaps some children find it difficult to reiterate received facts.

Although most primary teachers do divide their classes into groups, and this may appear more informal, there is a danger that we are merely presenting a variation on the didactic approach. This may be particularly true if the groups are always formed according to the ability of the children. Certainly, smaller groups can enable the teacher to target particular activities more effectively. Some groups can be 'low maintenance', being involved in self-correcting activities which require little or no supervision. The success of this approach depends on the organisational skills of the teacher in the selection of activities, in the way that the work is laid out, and in the way that progress of individuals is recorded. This method of working can be a mere organisational device.

The workshop approach

Some teachers aim to encourage children to work in groups in a collaborative way. The children are given tasks which enable them to identify and use their own experiences. Often they will be encouraged to pool their resources. In the process, they are enabled to articulate ideas, to identify and celebrate skills that they are using, and to see the relevance of these skills in other settings and in adult life. Whilst this form of group work helps to develop skills in decision-making and critical analysis, it can be too risky for some children. Any failure is very public. Individual needs may be ignored. Situations will arise where there seems to be no right or wrong answer and where assessing unpredictable outcomes is difficult. Research has shown that, although most of us feel that we are engaging the children in group work, this is not actually the case. A variety of reports provides evidence that children work individually for most of the time. Bennett (1985) sees the 'reality of groups as currently organised as a physical juxtaposition of individual pupils operating without a clear purpose or adequate management'. (British Journal of Educational Psychology: Monograph Series, 2 *Recent Advances in Classroom Research*, Scottish Academic Press.)

In this book, we are offering structured frameworks in the form of workshops, which acknowledge that primary school children are moving from an egocentric stage in their development towards one of awareness of their place in the classroom, the school, and beyond. We feel that it is important to examine our teaching strategies in order to enrich these broadening experiences. Richard Pring suggests that 'the transition between stages depends upon the sort of socialisation permitted or encouraged by the social institutions the child or youngster belongs to (say, family, school, church)'. (*Personal and Social Education in the Curriculum*, Hodder and Stoughton, 1989.)

Building confidence

Many of the ideas in this book are about developing confidence, which then provides the basis from which children are actively encouraged to take risks in the classroom. These risks are skills which can be taught: asking questions for clarification and information, challenging, being prepared to admit mistakes and recognising them as an integral part of the learning process, making decisions and informed choices. Implicit in this approach is the understanding that it is a developmental process which has to be congruent to the age of the child and to the stage which s/he has reached.

With confidence, which can be nurtured in the ethos of the classroom, children are able to put forward their ideas about the world. We offer practical ways of creating this ethos as well as processes which enable children to express their values and beliefs to each other. Through this, it is hoped that they will begin to understand the views of others and will appreciate that the world is not constructed according to their particular perspective.

Our methods encourage children to consider making choices, as options become more available to them during their primary years. In orchestrating experiences which develop respect for others, it is intended that a sense of self-worth is stimulated: we feel good about ourselves when we receive positive affirmation. Many of our activities encourage this.

A collaborative approach

Essential to the workshop approach is collaborative group work. Groups are varied and a range of activities is offered in Chapter 3. The aim is to allow children to have the experience of working with others, in order to develop social and academic skills. Groups are structured and restructured to enable children to learn as much as possible from and about each other. It is important to review ways in which they have worked together; for example, was the task completed? How well did it go? What were the problems? (A knowledge of group dynamics is a useful tool to develop the confidence of the teacher in directing group formations.)

Whilst we acknowledge that information is an important factor in sex education and personal development, we are concerned with other elements that influence our behaviour. In attempting to encourage children to consider particular lifestyles, we feel that it is essential to offer more than mere content. Here it is important to remember that primary school children have relatively little control over making their own choices; adults generally make decisions for them. Thus, in considering our approaches, we thought carefully about the parameters of choice and about how they change as the child gets older. Our priority has been to offer a climate which develops self-esteem. If we feel good about ourselves, we are more likely to consider what we do and how we do it.

Pages 22–26 are intended to enable teachers to consider approaches to the teaching of sex education and personal relationships. They may well be used to promote staff discussion about ways in which teachers go about helping children in this area.

1 Brainstorming our aims
What are the aims of teaching sex education and personal relationships?

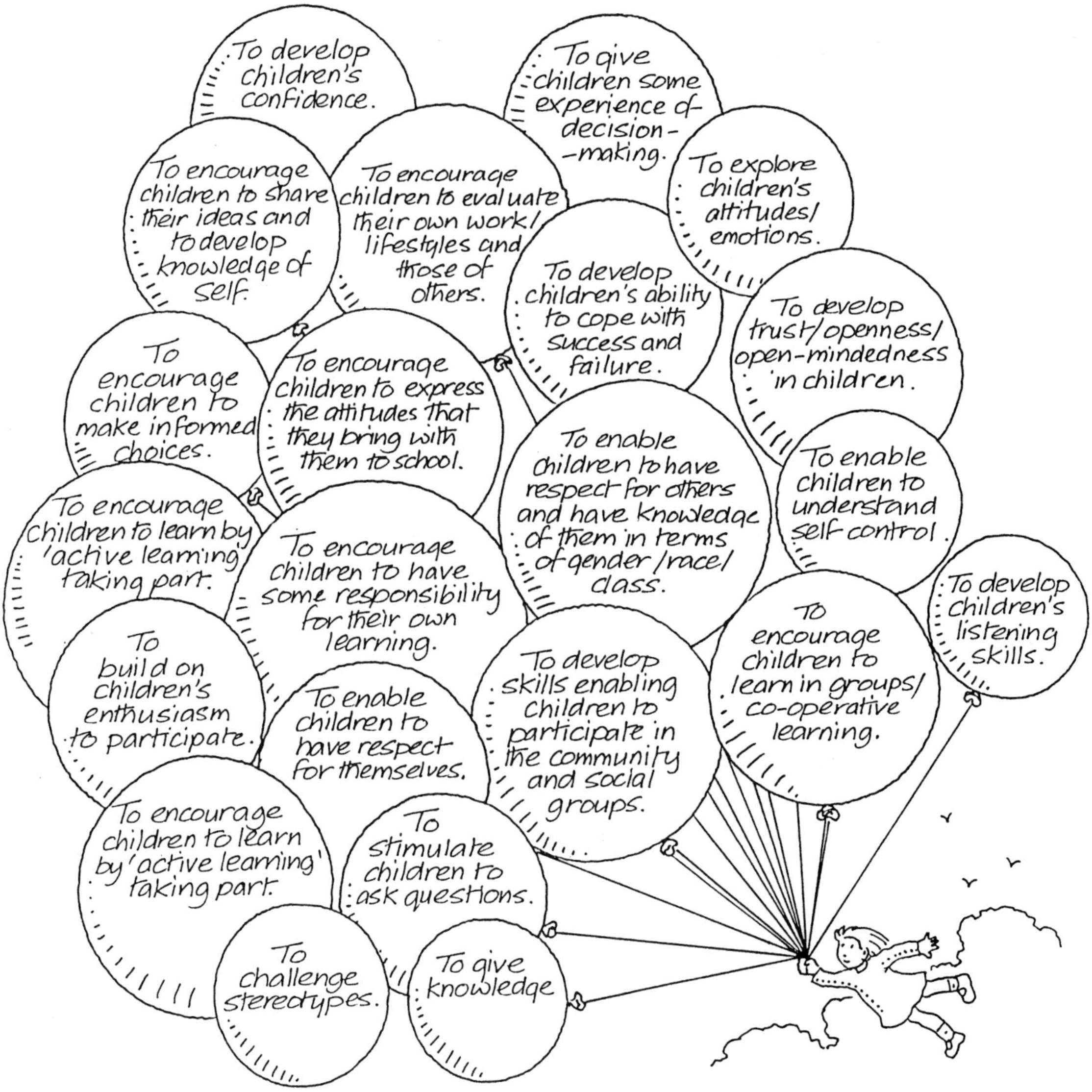

To develop children's confidence.

To give children some experience of decision-making.

To encourage children to share their ideas and to develop knowledge of self.

To encourage children to evaluate their own work/lifestyles and those of others.

To explore children's attitudes/emotions.

To develop children's ability to cope with success and failure.

To develop trust/openness/open-mindedness in children.

To encourage children to make informed choices.

To encourage children to express the attitudes that they bring with them to school.

To enable children to have respect for others and have knowledge of them in terms of gender/race/class.

To enable children to understand self-control.

To encourage children to learn by 'active learning' taking part.

To encourage children to have some responsibility for their own learning.

To develop children's listening skills.

To build on children's enthusiasm to participate.

To enable children to have respect for themselves.

To develop skills enabling children to participate in the community and social groups.

To encourage children to learn in groups/co-operative learning.

To encourage children to learn by 'active learning' taking part.

To stimulate children to ask questions.

To challenge stereotypes.

To give knowledge.

You may wish to add your own aims to this list. As a group, you may wish to prioritise the aims for your school.

2 Growing into group work
Some advantages and disadvantages of group work

Advantages

Can help with self-esteem.

Can encourage participation.

Values what the child has to say.

Encourages children to appreciate the needs of others.

Can be fun.

Encourages collaboration.

Encourages skills for adult life (see *ABC of children's skills* on p. 30).

It is relevant to the children's experiences and is based on these.

Can help with home/school links.

Encourages everybody to take part fully.

You may want to add your own points.

Disadvantages

May be an invasion of privacy.

May require a separate time in the school day to do it.

May de-skill some children because their failings might be very public.

May be threatening to the teacher.

Problem of teacher manipulation (transmission of own standards).

Potential problem of child assessment.

23

3 Chalk and talk

So what if I choose to teach about sex education and personal relationships by the 'chalk and talk' method?

Advantages	Disadvantages
Can be easy to do with large groups.	May not recognise the different stages at which children are.
Needs less space to do than group work.	May not motivate children.
Easy to assess whether children have learnt or not.	Gives the impression that there are right and wrong answers.
Easy to use experts.	Fails to use the experiences of children.
Aims can be clearer.	
Less contentious.	Does not encourage independence in children.
Teachers know clearly what is being transmitted.	May lead to opting out by the children.

You may wish to add your own points.

4 Teacher skills

In developing the skills of the children, what skills do we as teachers use?

In developing the children's skills, we use a whole variety of skills ourselves. When using group work methods our role may be slightly different to when we use other teaching styles. The emphasis for us is on:

- Encouraging.
- Valuing.
- Empathising.
- Listening.
- Negotiating.
- Contributing with care.
- Organising.
- Involving.
- Being sensitive.
- Being open.
- Being positive.
- Being flexible.
- Processing the learning.
- Making connections.
- Having respect for privacy.
- Being discreet.
- Helping children to appreciate each other's contributions.
- Being able to declare our purposes in a way which children can understand.
- Being consistent.
- Being able to cue children in and out sensitively.

You may wish to add your own ideas to the above list.

5 Role review

In working in this way, what is the role of the teacher?

- Not giving 'rights' and 'wrongs'.
- Allowing exploration of personal values (by providing a non-threatening, open climate).
- Enabling the child: sharing rather than directing and imposing.
- Being non-judgemental.
- Being as neutral as possible.
- Allowing children to learn through mistakes (mistakes are not failures).
- Allowing choices to be made.
- Involving children in the processes of learning (by planning, and evaluating).
- Providing resources.
- Providing a *positive* adult role: showing interest and respect.
- Recognising affective as well as cognitive learning (learning takes place through relationships).
- Seeing the importance of process and content.
- Showing trust.

☐ Language and sex

It is important that we as teachers come to terms with any difficulties which we have about language before we embark on sex education with our pupils. We want to avoid communicating any embarrassment, uneasiness, or any uncertainty about the terms that we use.

There are several points to be made here.

Do we want to make children aware that there may be different modes of language for talking about sex and sexuality? For instance, technical/medical words (penis, vagina, sexual intercourse), slang or vernacular words (fuck, cunt, screwing), and socially acceptable or euphemistic terms (making love, sleeping with, etc.).

People use different language to talk about the same thing, so it is vital to understand what the words mean. Otherwise difficulties and misconceptions are bound to arise.

It is vital that we are clear with children about the appropriateness of language in different situations. Some children will be accustomed to hearing sex talked about in 'street language', which we may decide is not appropriate for the classroom. We should, however, be non-judgemental about this.

We should not forget that words have associations for all of us, especially in the field of sex and sexuality. The words that we use, or hear being used, affect our attitudes and feelings to a considerable extent. We should not underestimate the power of language.

Teacher exercise on language and sex

The exercise on p. 28 is one which we have used extensively with teachers from primary and secondary schools in workshops and courses on sex education.

It could be used during a staff meeting or an INSET session on sex education. We have found that it really starts people talking, although it needs to be handled sensitively and explained thoroughly so that everyone understands what the exercise is about.

We have noticed that primary teachers seem to have more difficulty doing this exercise than secondary teachers. Why should this be? It could be to do with staff wanting to preserve the 'innocence' of younger children or else the fact that primary school staffs are always much smaller than in secondary schools, and so the embarrassment factor is more likely to come into play. We really do not have an answer.

Of course, the whole issue of language and sex needs to be taken into account in any discussion on sex education and should include parents and governors too.

6 Language and sex

Activity

The group is divided into three, equal subgroups: 3–5 people would be a good number. Each group has a large sheet of paper and a felt pen. The task is to brainstorm (without comment) all of the terms that people can think of for:

(a) female sexual organs,
(b) male sexual organs,
(c) sexual intercourse.

Each group covers one of the categories. Allow 5–10 minutes for this. Then each group passes their paper on to the next group, who add any more terms that they can think of. When each group has added their ideas to each category, the sheets of paper are displayed for the whole group to see.

Feedback

Each group should be given the chance to say how they felt about doing the activity. Then discussion can be widened to look at issues arising out of the work.

Trigger questions can include:

1 'How did you feel about doing the activity?'
2 'What do you notice about each list (looking at each one in turn)?'
3 'What kinds of words are there?'
4 'How could you group or classify them?'
5 'What does the use of language show us about our attitudes to sex?'
6 'How should all of this inform our work with children?'

☐ National Curriculum guidelines

Many of the activities in this book will enable the teacher to encourage the development of knowledge, skills and concepts which are required by the National Curriculum.

In using many of the 'workshop' ideas, a variety of skills will be learned and improved. To help you to identify these skills, we are offering an ABC of our own on p. 30. This may prove useful as a checklist for your evaluation of a lesson.

It is worth keeping in mind that skills can develop:

(a) the intellect,
(b) physical abilities,
(c) an appreciation of self,
(d) an appreciation of others.

At the time of writing, much of the National Curriculum has yet to be published, so we have not been able to relate activities to specific attainment targets. However, it is worth remembering that the National Curriculum as it stands relates to curriculum content. It is not difficult to relate the content of much of this book to attainment targets in the core subjects.

7 ABC of children's skills

Connecting
Affirming
Analysing
Concentrating

Anticipating
Arranging

Clarifying Conveying
Choosing Contributing
Copying
Checking out

Correcting
Creating
Comparing
Commentating

Co-ordinating
Describing
Decision-making
Directing

Empathising
Decoding
Deducing

Encouraging
Entertaining
Information sharing

Evaluating
Following
Guiding

Imagining
Explaining
Inspiring
Interpreting

Judging
Justifying
Leading

Listening
Learning
Negotiating

Numeracy
Predicting
Preparing

Problem–solving
Questioning
Reasoning

Recalling
Recording

Recounting
Reciprocating
Relating

Reflecting
Reporting back

Resolving
Reviewing

Simplifying
Selecting
Supporting

Summarising
Synthesising

Talking
Teaching

Transferring
Turn-taking

Valuing
Understanding
Visualising

Watching
Writing

8 Sex education workshop

This workshop is adaptable for use with teachers, parents and governors.

Ⓟ Purpose

To encourage an awareness of the breadth of sex education.

To share participants' own experiences of sex education and to use these to inform about the needs of a primary school child.

To identify and prioritise issues concerning sex education for future reference.

To identify and prioritise what children need to know about sex education and personal relationships when they leave primary school.

◐ Approximate timing

60 minutes.

Introduction

This is to welcome the participants and to outline the purposes of the session. It is a good idea to remind participants that the work is going to involve them in an active way.

Ice-breaker

This is always a good idea. It helps participants to engage with each other.

You may wish to choose an Ice-breaker that you know. We have found 'Human bingo' useful for focusing on issues (see pp. 37–40).

Drawing on participants' experiences

In groups of three or four, ask participants to talk about their experiences of sex education at school.

Was it what they needed at the time?

Did it prepare them for later?

Feedback

This enables participants to share any thoughts from the previous activity.

Personal reflection time

This is to enable participants to respond individually to a checklist.

You will need to photocopy the appropriate checklist (see pp. 34–36) and ensure that each participant has a pen or pencil.

Of course, you can mix and match the statements from each of the checklists or, ideally, make up your own.

Sharing the checklist

Initially, it is valuable to do this in smaller groups of two or four.

An activity such as 'All change' (see p. 43) will enable participants to work within a different group setting.

Feedback

This will give an opportunity for the whole group to share ideas and comments from the small groups.

Brainstorm

This free-flow activity will enable the whole group to express their feelings about issues arising from the checklist. The group leader records all ideas, having first asked the question:

'What issues have been raised for you so far?'

Alternative brainstorm

An alternative brainstorm might be:

'What do children need to know about sex education and personal relationships by the time that they leave primary school?'

Prioritisation activity

Some issues raised will be more important than others. Some will need to be looked at in the longer term. A prioritisation activity will allow all of the issues to be sorted and grouped. This should be done in small groups.

Feedback

This will allow the group leader to list the priorities of the participants and will inform the policy-making process.

Closing activity

Ideally this will be designed to evaluate the session. See ideas for evaluation in Chapter 3.

8 Checklist for teachers

The workshop leader will tell you how long you have to complete this checklist by yourself. You will then have the opportunity to discuss it with one or two other people.

Agree   Disagree

It is important for the school to deal with sex education, since parents find it very hard to handle the subject for themselves.

We should deal with sex education only when children ask questions.

There are not enough resources around for teaching sex education.

Sex education should be taught only by those confident enough to do it.

There is a place for working with single-sex groups in sex education.

I do not know enough about certain aspects to be able to teach sex education.

I feel that we might be going against the culture of the home if we teach sex education.

I worry about the time that it will take for all of the staff to reach a consensus about sex education.

If we do not provide a sex education programme, children will invent their own explanations.

Teaching about sex education in its broadest context would involve me looking at my methodology.

8 Checklist for parents

The workshop leader will tell you how long you have to complete this checklist by yourself. You will then have the opportunity to discuss it with one or two other people.

	Agree	**Disagree**
I should prefer to deal with sex education myself rather than leave it to a teacher.		
I feel that there is no place for teaching about sexually transmitted diseases in primary schools.		
I believe that sex education can encourage children to make responsible decisions about relationships.		
Informing children about sexual matters at an early stage will make them less self-conscious about it later.		
If teachers teach about sex education, children will take it seriously.		
A sex education programme should involve looking at male/female attitudes to sex and sexuality.		
I feel that children should have a thorough knowledge of how their bodies work.		
I feel that some areas of people's sexual behaviour should not be discussed in school.		
Young people today need to know more about sex than when I was at school.		
I feel that sex education should be taught in the context of the family.		

8 Checklist for governors

The workshop leader will tell you how long you have to complete this checklist by yourself. You will then have the opportunity to discuss it with one or two other people.

	Agree	Disagree
Sex education is about developing confidence.		
Sex education is about developing responsibility.		
Sex education is about assertion.		
Sex education is about allowing children to learn about bodily functions.		
Sex education is about learning about the dangers of AIDS and sexually transmitted diseases.		
Sex education is about developing self-esteem.		
Sex education is about widening children's awareness of sexual expression.		
Sex education is about encouraging children to be aware of their own feelings, and those of others.		
Sex education is about learning that people can enjoy their own sexuality.		
Sex education is about understanding the dangers of exploitation.		

9 Human bingo

Purpose

To encourage participants to mingle and get to know each other, at the same time focusing on some of the issues to be developed in the workshop.

What to do

Photocopy grid sheets (see pp. 38–40), one for each person. Distribute them, explaining that each person must try to put someone else's name in each square by asking the person if the statement relates to him/her. If the answer is YES, the participant writes that person's name in the square. If NO, the participant moves on to someone else.

Everyone stands up and asks each other at the same time. This activity can go on for a long time, but we suggest a time limit of 10 minutes.

This is a good way of mixing the group. When you ask people to stop, you can ask them to work in pairs with the person nearest to them. Alternatively, you can put numbers or colours on the back of the sheets so that people join up with the person who has the corresponding number or colour.

When partners are paired off, ask them to sit down together. Provide trigger questions:

'Why do you think that the statements were chosen?'
'What have they to do with sex education?'
'Would you have chosen different statements?'

Allow 5 minutes for this, and another 5 minutes for feedback to the whole group.

The whole activity should take 20–25 minutes.

9 Human bingo: suggested statements for teachers

Someone who had formal lessons about sex education at primary school.

Someone who has used a school nurse to help them with teaching about sex education.

Someone who has used a TV programme about sex education.

Someone who has difficulty with boys and girls changing for P.E.

Someone who has read a romance story in a magazine.

Someone who has difficulty with slang words about sex.

Someone who thinks it is the parents' job to teach about sex.

Someone who would not feel happy about talking about HIV and AIDS with children.

9 Human bingo: suggested statements for parents

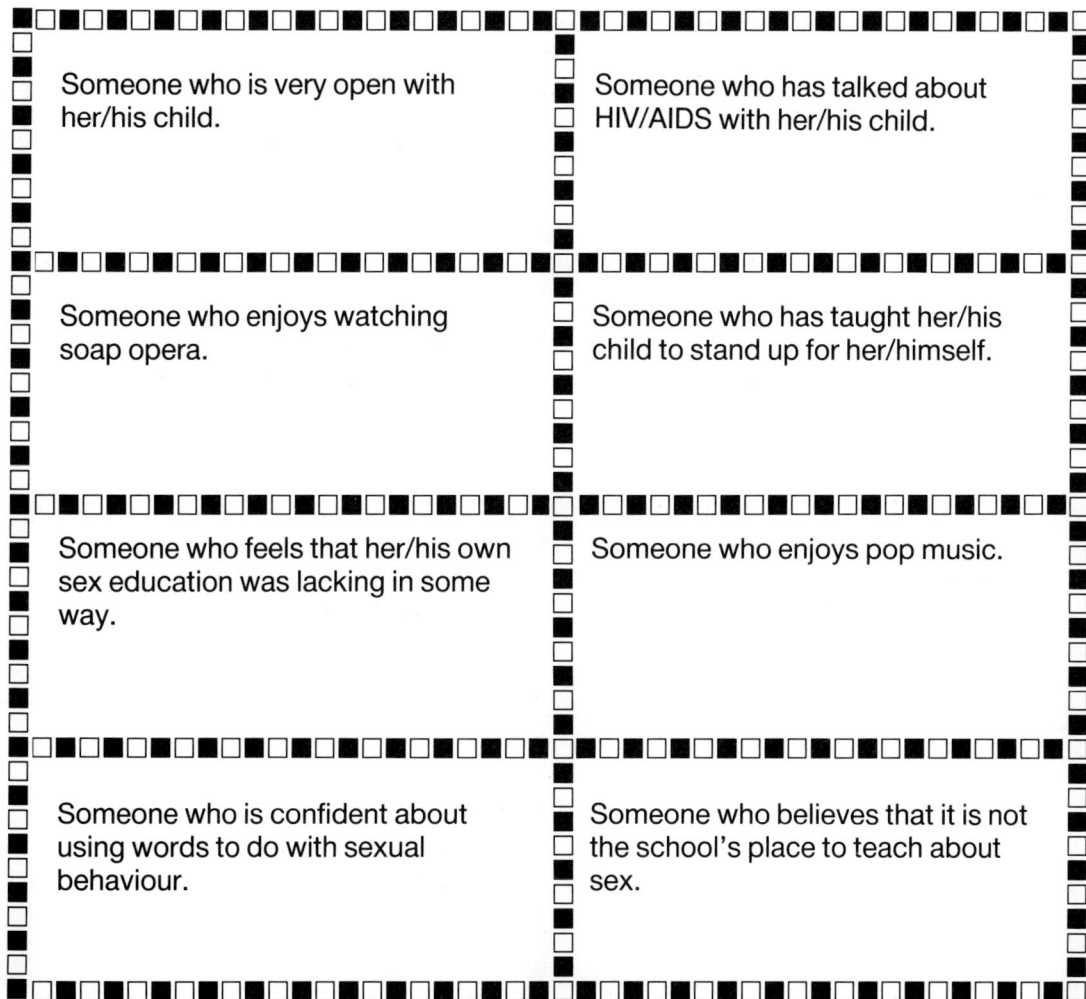

Someone who is very open with her/his child.

Someone who has talked about HIV/AIDS with her/his child.

Someone who enjoys watching soap opera.

Someone who has taught her/his child to stand up for her/himself.

Someone who feels that her/his own sex education was lacking in some way.

Someone who enjoys pop music.

Someone who is confident about using words to do with sexual behaviour.

Someone who believes that it is not the school's place to teach about sex.

9 Human bingo: suggested statements for governors

Someone who had formal sex education at primary school.	Someone who feels that sex education will prevent unwanted pregnancies.
Someone who feels that looking at 'Page 3' girls does no harm to anyone.	Someone who feels that teaching about reproduction is enough.
Someone who sees assertion as part of a sex education programme.	Someone who enjoys watching a TV soap opera.
Someone who feels it is better to leave sex education until children ask questions about it.	Someone who feels that a sex education programme might offend some parents.

·3·

Making it happen

The next section is full of ideas that are easily adapted to a variety of situations. The activities are designed to promote co-operative learning and a classroom atmosphere which involves the children and allows them to express their values.

We are aware that children who are not used to working in different groups may exhibit behaviour which is not conducive to a collaborative model. We are also aware that some teachers are used to a more formal approach. We therefore suggest that teachers and children who are not used to working in such a way should approach a 'workshop model' gradually. For example, the idea of a 'brainstorm' is a very easy activity to begin with.

We have found that teachers, as they become more confident about working in this way, devise all kinds of new ideas for themselves. They come to value this approach and are pleasantly surprised by the positive engagement that results from group work.

10 ABC of workshop ideas

Agendas

These may be offered to structure the way in which groups think through a particular set of issues. We find it useful to list them publicly, even if there are only two or three items. It is valuable for the group to have ownership of its own agenda and this can lead to prioritisation.

'Aha!'

Books may be distributed to the children and labelled 'Aha' books. Their purpose should be to enable the children to record in writing or pictures specific moments of learning. Or they could be used whenever the child wants to write down questions that come into focus for her/him.

Teachers might choose to have an 'Aha' box in the classroom for the children to 'post' any ideas, suggestions or queries.

Large, blank pieces of paper, labelled 'Aha', may be displayed on the wall for some time. Here the children can publicly display their ideas.

'All change'

This is a quick activity to enable the children to work in new groups. The class should be sitting in a circle. The teacher asks the class to stand up, then asks those who are wearing a particular colour to change places with each other.

This may be followed by any other criterion chosen by either the teacher or a child (for example, people who had breakfast today, those who played football at playtime). The criteria for exchanging places can vary. The teacher might choose statements which are related to specific points of knowledge, such as those children who know how long it takes for a baby to grow before it is born. The knowledge can then be checked out. This is a good way of assessing the success of a particular session. A good statement is, 'All change if you have learned something new today', followed by, 'What did you learn?'

The 'All change' activity may be used to encourage children to reflect on their feelings about a particular session. In this way a teacher might be able to evaluate the children's enjoyment: 'All change if you enjoyed something about this afternoon', followed by, 'What did you enjoy?'

In our experience, this activity should last for only a short time.

Animal noises

This is an activity in which the teacher has a pile of cards with repeated images or names of four or five animals. The cards are distributed to the children, who are asked, at a given signal, to produce the noise of their particular animal. This is a funny and noisy way of forming four or five groups.

Brainstorms

Brainstorms are triggered by questions.

Brainstorming is a well-known technique which, from our experience, is often abused. The idea of a brainstorm is to allow children to suggest anything at all, which is then publicly recorded on a flipchart or chalkboard, *without any discussion at that point*. The whole purpose of a brainstorm is to allow the group to 'wander free' with their ideas. Lots of lateral thinking emerges if brainstorms are used correctly. The discussion of ideas follows a brainstorm.

It is very tempting for teachers to censor seemingly disconnected words. We have found that it is very hard to appear non-judgemental about some suggestions.

Again, this is a quick activity. It might be an idea to set targets or time limits.

Buzz group

Buzz groups are small groups which are formed from the large group. The purpose of forming such groups is to enable all participants to contribute. Buzz groups can be given short, timed tasks to perform. The buzz group can then be encouraged to 'feed back' to the whole group.

Carousel

There are two types of Carousel which we would recommend for use with primary aged children. Both types may involve problem-solving and information/experience-sharing. It is advisable to give very clear, concise instructions when setting up Carousels.

(a) The leader divides the class into three groups of equal size. Ideas for doing this are included in this section. Each group is given a different task, e.g. something to read and discuss. A time limit is set for this. Towards the end of the time, the leader numbers off participants (e.g. ABC), starting with one group and repeating for the other two. At a given moment all of the A's are asked to form a new group, as are all of the B's and C's. In the new groups, the children are instructed to share their discussions from the previous group. This is a very efficient way of synthesising information and experiences. If it is thought necessary, the teacher might decide to have a whole class discussion to identify the learning that has taken place.

(b) The class is divided into groups of, say, eight children. Four children sit opposite the other four in a row. The teacher sets a time limit for the pairs to discuss a given situation, whether it be a role play, a problem to solve, or an issue to discuss. At the end of the given time, one row of four is asked to move on one place, so that new pairs are formed. This enables the children to have another perspective on the same situation. This can be repeated up to three times in this configuration. The teacher may choose to have larger groups to set up the Carousel.

Case studies

Case studies are useful means by which to develop discussions. A group of children might be presented with a short piece of writing which describes people's behaviour in certain situations. The children read this together. Trigger questions are offered to encourage them to reflect and present their ideas to each other.

Children can be encouraged to write simple case studies for each other, along with trigger questions. These can even be done in strip cartoon form.

We have found that case studies which present a 'cliff-hanger' type of situation are particularly valuable to initiate dialogue.

As with many activities in this book, we are encouraging children to see the world from another perspective.

Checklist

Sometimes children need to be guided through an activity or to be reminded of things that they should be doing or looking out for. This is the purpose of a checklist. It can be written up on the board or given out as a handout. For example, if the class is preparing to receive a visitor, the checklist might say:

How will the room be arranged?
Who will welcome the visitor?
Who will ask the first question?

Checklists can be devised by the children themselves.

Circles

To ensure that children sit in a circle may seem obvious but it is the only way that we know of where children can see each other and can become more aware of body language. We always try to sit at the same level as the children, in order to achieve a sense of equality within the group. This may prove difficult in crowded classrooms but we feel so strongly about this configuration that we always make sure that a 'circle space' is available, not only for 'workshop' times but also for story-telling, news-times, etc.

Contracts

The idea of establishing contracts or ground-rules is one way of ensuring that the class has responsibility for monitoring its own behaviour. The process can be started by brainstorming as a whole group. The question might be, 'If we are to work together as a class, what rules do we need?' Suggestions from the children might include listening to each other; making sure that we do not talk at the same time; having the right to 'pass', etc. Following the brainstorm, it might well be necessary to initiate small-group discussions, exploring whether the ground-rules are viable or not.

Some teachers have established contracts with children at the beginning of a school year and the contracts have been put on display in the classroom. It is a good idea to review contracts from time to time.

Data collection

This is an important process in dealing with the exploration of personal relationships. Children enjoy compiling and using questionnaires. However, it is important to remember that these can be time-consuming activities and that there is a danger that the class can move from an educational pursuit to a recreational one.

In constructing the agenda for the data, the children should be made aware of the rights of others to privacy and of the need to have as near to value-free approaches as they can.

Information may be recorded in a variety of forms, such as bar charts, pie charts, graphs.

Debriefs

Debriefs are very important. Without them, much of the learning will be lost. By debriefing the activity, the children are encouraged to reflect on what they have understood or on how they felt about the experience that they have had.

Debriefs may be organised so that they involve small group discussions or individual responses. Outcomes of the debrief may be spoken or written down. Useful debrief questions are:

'What did you learn?'
'How are you feeling now?'
'What are the three most important facts that you remember?'
'How will you use what you have learned today?'

Feedback

This is an essential part of any lesson or workshop, whereby people working in smaller groups are enabled to report on what they did or learned to the larger group.

Graffiti wall

This method of evaluation may be used at the end of a lesson or at the end of the day.

A large piece of paper, prepared to look like a brick wall, is placed on the wall. Children are told that they can write any comments about the activity that they have just done on this sheet of paper. Comments are, of course, anonymous. Teachers who feel comfortable with a group will welcome both positive and negative comments.

We have found it useful to have an area of the classroom as a semi-permanent graffiti display. The children are more likely to use it when there is no pressure on them to do so.

Children can be encouraged to write 'graffiti responses' on individual pieces of paper, which they then attach to the 'wall'. This discourages copying of other people's ideas.

Grids

Grids are useful for encouraging children to talk to each other.

Each participant is given an identical piece of paper which has been divided into a number of sections. Each section will have a category (e.g. 'Someone who knows what "puberty" means', followed by a space and then by: 'What does it mean?'). The children are asked to stand up and question each other in an attempt to find someone who can answer each particular category. The idea is to fill up the grid.

The categories may concern anything that is relevant to what is being taught at the time.

Ice-breaker

Sometimes called a 'warm-up', this is any activity at the start of a session which encourages people to start thinking or moving. It is particularly important to use this in groups where the people are new to each other or do not know each other very well. Even if people do know each other well, ice-breakers are excellent for ensuring that they behave co-operatively.

Interviews (the 'Visitor experience')

This strategy departs from the traditional idea of having someone come into the classroom in the role of 'expert' on some subject or another. In this activity, children help to decide whom they would like to ask into school, why they want them to come, and what they are going to ask them.

The idea is to involve the whole class, so that as many children as possible will suggest questions to ask; some will go to welcome the visitor when s/he arrives at school, and will bring her/him into the classroom, etc.

Obviously, the older the children, the more responsibility that they can take for the session. However, it must be remembered that the more we 'own' something, the more we will obtain from the experience.

Introductions

It may seem obvious but we need to remember to give children an overview of what a particular session is about. It helps to demystify the learning process. The introduction to a session will enable the children to know the purpose of the session and in what ways they will be working in the allocated time.

Jigsaw pictures

Jigsaw pictures, or statements, are useful in forming groups. The teacher should have a picture or else a written instruction or piece of information, which is cut into pieces. The number of pieces into which the 'trigger' is cut will determine the size of the group. Of course, the teacher will need to have several to photocopy if small groups are required.

A piece of the jigsaw is given to each child. The children must seek out others to form a whole. They may then be given a task relating to the picture or statement.

Line-ups

This activity involves children in forming lines in particular patterns. For instance, with the instruction, 'Line up according to the month of the year in which you were born', the teacher might need to indicate which end of the room is January and which is December. Another activity might be lining up according to age (from oldest to youngest). The teacher should be sensitive to the feelings of children in asking them to line up according to certain criteria, such as height.

Line-ups may be done in silence so that the children have to invent a code to communicate.

Once in line, the children may then be divided into new groups according to where they are standing. In a class where real trust has been developed, the children could be asked to line up according to the contributions that they have made to a particular session, e.g. those who have talked a lot, those who have talked a little. In this way they are encouraged to analyse their involvement in group work.

Matching

This is a way of forming pairs or small groups. The teacher may distribute a variety of pictures and ask children who have the same picture to form groups. The process of doing this can be a learning experience too. The teacher may distribute some words and pictures to the children and ask them to match the words to the pictures. Similarly, animals and their young may be used. Other matching ideas might be shapes or paper of different colours. Whatever is matched can be used as a trigger for the activity that follows, once the groups have been formed.

Mill and grab

This is a quick, energising activity. All participants must be standing up. The teacher asks children to form groups very quickly according to a variety of criteria, e.g. 'Join with someone who wears the same colour as you; likes your favourite colour TV programme'.

This process is very useful for reforming groups to enable children to work with people whom they would not necessarily choose for themselves.

Milling

After an intensive piece of work, it is a good idea for the children to mill around actively. This provides an energising opportunity for them to explore each group's work. While they are still on their feet, the teacher may wish to interject with questions such as, 'What have you learned from looking at other people's work?' or 'Did other people have the same kind of ideas?'

Mixing

Mixing is an important aspect of group work. Left to their own devices, children will tend to work only with their friends. Of course, this is valid from time to time. However, it is beneficial for them to experience working with people whom they would not necessarily choose. By doing this, it is possible for them to come to appreciate people's qualities, and this can lead to heightened awareness of others. There is a variety of suggestions in this and other chapters on how to encourage mixing.

Name games

Many games may be used to introduce children or adults to each other, say at the start of a new school year or a workshop. They are best done sitting in a circle. Two such examples are as follows.

(a) One person starts by saying, 'I'm John'. The person next to him says, 'I'm Barbara, and this is John'. The next person says, 'I'm Fazal, and this is Barbara and this is John', and so on.

(b) A large piece of paper is placed on the floor in the centre of the circle or else is displayed on a wall. Each person takes it in turn to sign their name (with a big felt-tipped pen) and to say something about their name, e.g. 'My name is Frank, but everyone calls me Frankie'.

Numbering off

One way to group children is to number them off around the class. If you want there to be five groups, number children in turn, 1–2–3–4–5, 1–2–3–4–5, etc. Then ask all the 1s to form a group, then the 2s, 3s, and so on until everyone is in a group. With younger children, use names of things, e.g. fruit – peach, pear, apple, orange, banana – or parts of the body – foot, hand, elbow, nose, ears.

'Pass'

In group activities, where everyone takes it in turn to say something, it can sometimes be worrying or even frightening for children to be put on the spot. You need to establish right from the start, therefore, that everyone has the right to miss a turn, or 'pass', and that s/he will be given the chance to make a contribution at the end of the round.

Public recording

In a classroom where the sharing of ideas is encouraged and where everyone's contribution is valued, it is a good idea to adopt the habit of recording everything that comes out of class discussions in a way which can be seen and acknowledged by the whole class. The teacher need not do it all the time; children can do it too. It vastly improves everybody's listening and writing skills!

Questions

Some questions will encourage children to think in a creative way whilst others will not. For example, questions with the words 'How?', 'Why?' and 'In what ways?' are open-ended, whereas those beginning with 'What?', or 'When?' may produce simple responses which do not develop discussion. Skilled teachers will select the moment to intervene when children are working in small groups and are more likely to offer open-ended questions which lead on the thinking.

When two or more questions are being considered by children working in groups, it is a good idea to list them.

Quiet times (reflection)

In the busy primary school day, it can be easy to forget the necessity for short periods of time to enable children to reflect on their learning and their feelings. We have found that trigger questions are useful for facilitating children's thinking about what the learning process means for them. For example, a teacher might say, 'I'd like you to stop for a moment and look at the work you've just done and think how you feel about it.'

Role play

Most children enjoy pretending games. Role-play activities allow them to explore what it is like to be somebody else. Role-play situations may either be devised by the children themselves or offered by the teacher. Activities may be done in pairs, in small groups, or as a whole class. The benefits of role play may be completely lost unless followed by debrief questions such as, 'How did it feel to be . . .?' or 'Did you think so and so was right to do . . .?'

Rounds

There are times, often at the end of a lesson, when it is valuable for everyone in the class to gather together, perhaps after working in small groups, and to share their ideas and feelings about what has just happened. The teacher invites everyone to take it in turns – it helps if you can be in a circle – to complete a 'sentence stem', e.g. 'One thing I've learned today is . . .' or 'The best thing about this morning was . . .'. It is probably best to keep it very simple when you start using this technique but, as the children become used to doing it, you can introduce more varied aspects, e.g. 'The thing I'd like to know more about next time is . . .', or more affective comments such as, 'One word which sums up how I feel is . . .'. Of course, you must stress that anyone may 'pass' who wants to.

Scribe

This is the 'secretary' who writes down the ideas within a group. In small groups, children may need to be appointed to be scribes. Otherwise a system of sharing must be introduced by the teacher. One way of doing this is by numbering off the children and, after a few minutes, calling out a number to change the scribe/leader of each group.

In classes where some children find it difficult to write, the children may be partnered to help each other. Obviously, this is a sensitive issue, and intimate knowledge of the group will inform the teacher's approach.

Silence

In periods of silence, we should not think that, just because no one is speaking, nothing is going on. Silence is extremely important, when working with groups of children or adults, for allowing reflection to take place. We find it useful to ask children to close their eyes so that they can focus more intensely on whatever the content may be.

Trigger

A trigger is something which is used to start off an activity. This may be almost anything: a suggestion, an idea, an object, a poem, a picture, part of a video. It works well only if the subsequent questions are able to develop or open up ideas arising from the trigger.

Turn-taking

It is often very hard for young children to await their turn and so they start to talk at the same time. To encourage them to take turns, teachers may wish to use a bean-bag: only the person with the bean-bag may talk. Of course, the teacher must ensure that the bean-bag is shared equitably.

Another idea is for the teacher to use a small ball of string. This activity must take place in a circle. When one child has contributed, the teacher holds on to the end of the string and passes the ball on to the person who has spoken. When the next person has finished, the first speaker passes the ball on to him/her whilst still holding on to the string. The ball is passed on after every speaker. To untangle the string, the last person who has it is asked to recall one idea given by the person before him/her. The children take it in turns until the entire string is returned to the teacher.

Labelling children A, B, C, or 1, 2, 3, and then giving them a task encourages turn-taking when each letter or number is given a set time by the teacher: for example A's in each group talks about . . . for one minute . . . Now it's B's turn for one minute.'

By using a deck of cards, the teacher may encourage turn-taking by requesting that a child with a certain card talks first, followed by someone with a different card. Of course, there are many variations on this idea.

Verbal tennis

This activity encourages children to come up with 'quick-fire' associated words. To do it, they need to work in pairs. The teacher gives a category (e.g. girls' names). One of the pair starts by giving a word which fits into the category, and her/his partner then has to say a different word, which still fits into the given category. At intervals, the teacher should change the category. This continues until the teacher stops the activity. Every pair does it at the same time and the children should have no more than 30–40 seconds with each category.

Verbal tennis is useful to trigger off discussion. For example, the teacher might ask the children to try out male jobs, or female jobs. This can lead to a discussion on stereotyping.

You might choose to use it to recap on words concerned with parts of the body.

It is also a good evaluative tool. You may choose to offer the category, 'words which describe the work we have just done together'.

11 Evaluation: how was it for you?

We recommend that workshop sessions include an evaluation because it not only indicates to the children that their feelings and thoughts are important but also encourages them to reflect on what they have done and learned. It can lead to a better understanding of feelings and can encourage children to appreciate that they have the right to express criticism in a positive way. Evaluative activities can inform the teacher about the success or otherwise of particular sessions.

At some stage, self-evaluation can be introduced. We have found that it is best to encourage positive responses. Often children and adults find it difficult to acknowledge or even recognise their own achievements.

All of the evaluation activities can lead to further discussion which may be carried out in large or small groups or individually. Questions act as triggers:

'Why do you feel this way?'
'What went well/badly?'
'What did you do well?'
'What might you do differently next time?'
'What did you find out about yourself/others?'

It is a good idea to gather a large repertoire of evaluation techniques. Otherwise, the children may devalue their purpose. We have found that it is useful to indicate to the children that their ideas are important. This can be shown in a variety of ways such as:

'I remember from last time that some of you felt . . .'
'I've decided to try a new way of going about . . . because of what some of you said (indicated) . . .'
'You all seemed to enjoy . . . so I thought we'd . . .'

Many of the evaluation activities are a public display and this may lead to a situation where either children avoid expressing their true feelings in front of their peers or they may simply copy, or do the opposite of, another child or group of children. These situations can be a point of discussion, and a real learning experience. It is important to remember that honest responses are more likely to happen in a situation where the classroom climate is one of mutual trust.

— Some evaluation activities —

1 The children can be asked to draw a face to express how they feel.

2 The children might be asked to stand at a height which states how they feel about the session: low down would indicate not very good, and very tall would signal very good indeed.

3 The teacher might ask the children to express their feelings by a facial expression.

4 The children can show their reactions by using the arm as a 'barometer'. At right angles, they could show that they feel good and by stretching their arm outwards, they could express their negative feelings.

5 The teacher might choose to do a finger and thumb count. Ten would equal excellent, whereas one would indicate that the children did not enjoy the session.

6 The teacher can ask the children to devise their own codes to express feelings. This may lead into a discussion about body language.

7 The teacher might have a list of words that describe feelings, which is displayed and added to over a number of weeks. The teacher might ask the children to choose a word to describe how they feel.

8 The children can indicate their feelings by a thumbs up, thumbs in the middle, or thumbs down.

9 Line-ups can be useful as an evaluation (see p.49).

10 Fire alarm evaluation is an activity where the children are asked to line up at the door and metaphorically to take with them the three most important things that they have learned so far that day – what they would save in the event of a fire.

11 Musical evaluation is where half of the group stands still whilst the other half moves to a piece of music. When the music stops, the moving group stop and talk to the person(s) nearest to them. The teacher would 'feed in'.

☐ The 'Visitor experience'

Primary schools are traditionally full of people who are not officially on the payroll: parents who have come in to help with reading; visitors who have come to talk to the head or other teachers; people delivering supplies; administrators, advisers, Inspectors from the Education Office – the list is endless. Although it is often not acknowledged, children and visitors alike gain much from the interactions which occur throughout the day, both in and out of the classroom.

When it comes to sex education, primary schools have often turned to people outside the school, asking them to come in and 'do' various topics, the classic case being the school nurse or health visitor who comes in to talk about menstruation with the 10–11 year old girls. Even when the boys are included, there is sometimes a reluctance to talk about the issues and so a film or slide show may be used instead.

Where a visitor is used for this kind of work, it is unusual for them to be involved in the planning of the work. Often they are insufficiently briefed about the children with whom they will be working (their background, levels of knowledge, etc.) or about the work that they are expected to do (the aims, objectives, teaching methods, etc.). Apart from all this, what kind of messages are teachers giving to children about sex when we are seen to opt out and to bring in someone else to do the job for us? Surely it just reinforces the idea that sex is something that is embarrassing and not fit to be talked about in polite circles? Furthermore, facts about sex are often seen to be the province of the medical profession. Not everyone acknowledges that the feelings about sex are just as important as the facts.

Dr Leslie Button's work on using visitors in the classroom was part of his important project on Developmental Group Work with adolescents, which first emerged in the late 1970s. It recognised that the 'Visitor experience' can play a very important part in the personal growth and development of young people by giving them not only access to outside expertise and information but also the opportunity to prepare for and look after a visitor, thus taking responsibility for their own learning. Children new to this experience will need support from the teacher, who must ensure that all of the children are playing a part in the 'Visitor experience'. (Button, L., *Developmental Group Work with Adolescents* Hodder and Stoughton)

How many of us have, in different situations, sat through a visiting speaker's lecture in a passive manner, with all kinds of things going through our minds? Why did they invite this person to come? I could think of better and more appropriate speakers! Why do they not ask us what *we* think? I would like to challenge him/her on that! What on earth is s/he going on about? Thus, we may emerge from potentially useful and exciting opportunities, feeling bored and frustrated. How much better to have been *actively* involved in planning and preparing for the visitor, so that we get what we want from the session, and it is our agenda, not just that of the visitor, which is being addressed.

Process and content

When we use the 'Visitor experience' in the primary school, we need to be clear that two things will be happening at the same time:

1   The children will be going through a *process* containing many different opportunities for learning: how to write letters/make a phone call, working out a timetable or schedule, organising refreshments, thinking up questions, putting things in a logical order, greeting and thanking people.

2   The children will gather information and *content* in the course of the visit.

It is very important that we remain aware of these two aspects.

You might like to consider inviting into the classroom:

(a)   a pregnant mum, or a dad,
(b)   a health visitor,
(c)   the school nurse,
(d)   a doctor,
(e)   a new parent.

12 The 'Visitor experience'

Ⓟ Purpose

To decide, as a class, on an appropriate visitor.

To generate questions to ask the visitor.

To identify roles of individual class members before, during and after the visit.

To identify the visitor's needs and ways of meeting these.

＞ Suggested age range

Any age.

∥ Materials needed

Photocopies of Visitor checklist (see p. 62), flipchart or board.

◕ Approximate timing

Preparation: 45 – 60 minutes minimum.

Visitor time: approx. 30 minutes, depending on attention span of the children.

▶ What else it relates to

Adaptable to many activities in this book.

👥 Numbers involved

Whole class.

What to do
---

1 Process

The teacher explains that the class is going to learn about a particular aspect of sex education (e.g. menstruation, how babies are cared for). The whole class can then brainstorm, 'Who might be able to tell us about this?' After a discussion, a vote can be taken on the most suitable person.

Once the decision is made, the Visitor checklist can be used. Alternatively, each class member can generate his/her own list on how to look after the visitor from start to finish. This will involve trigger questions such as:

Who will invite the visitor and how will they do it?

How will the visitor get here?

The class will need to plan for the whole time that the visitor will be in the school building.

2   Content

You might want to ask the class to work in pairs and to think of questions to ask the visitor. These questions can then be shared by the whole class, then prioritised. After this, individual children can be allocated a question. Those children who are not involved in asking questions might be responsible for recording the answers. Others will be involved in the process in different ways, e.g. greeting the visitor, keeping time, explaining to the visitor how this work fits in with what they have been doing, thanking the visitor, showing him/her in and out of the room.

At the end of the questioning, it is a good idea to have a child who will ask the visitor if s/he has said everything that s/he wanted to say. Also it is important for the children to have feedback from the visitor about how s/he felt about the visit.

Later, as soon as possible after the visitor has gone, the children need to share how they felt about the visit, their roles, and what they learned, and to consider what they might want to feed back to the visitor. This could be a photocopy of the work that comes out of it or simply a 'Thank you' card.

12 Visitor checklist

OUR VISITOR IS ....

WE SHALL MEET HIM/HER AT .... (time/place)

S/HE WILL BE STAYING FOR .... MINUTES

WE SHALL OFFER REFRESHMENTS IN .... (place)

MY SUGGESTED PLAN OF THE ROOM FOR THE VISIT IS ....

....

....

Who will do what?   (This might involve more than one person.)

.... WILL COLLECT THE VISITOR.

.... WILL OFFER REFRESHMENTS.

.... WILL INTRODUCE THE VISITOR.

.... WILL KEEP TIME.

.... WILL TAKE NOTES.

.... WILL ASK THE FIRST QUESTION.

.... WILL CLOSE THE VISIT.

.... WILL ASK THE VISITOR IF THERE IS
                   ANYTHING ELSE S/HE WANTS TO SAY.

.... WILL ASK HOW THE VISITOR IS FEELING.

.... WILL THANK THE VISITOR.

.... WILL TAKE THE VISITOR OUT.

Can you think of any other jobs to be done?

....

....

....

....

....

....

....

·4·
Knowing me, knowing you

Activities in this section are designed to help children to develop self-awareness and respect for others. We believe that people should try to accept themselves and others for who and what they are. These ideas, along with those that you may develop yourself, will help to lead children to the realisation that we need to take responsibility for our own lives.

The activities will help children to:

- Identify personal qualities.
- Appreciate that variety is an essential part of life, and that we may all have different values.
- Consider how they are perceived by others.
- Celebrate skills.
- Enhance a sense of self-identity.
- Understand the difference between needs and wants.
- Analyse their feelings and actions.
- Recognise the right to personal safety.
- Explore assumptions and variations in lifestyles.

13 Who am I?

(P) **Purpose**

To analyse personal characteristics.
To develop self-awareness and confidence.

> **Suggested age range**

Upper Infants and above.

//// **Materials needed**

Photocopies of worksheet on p. 66, art materials.

◑ **Approximate timing**

30 minutes.

▶ **What else it relates to**

The ABC of personal qualities
My personal coat of arms
A collage of me
Different parts of me
What I need/What I want
Graphing out our needs and wants
My ideal day

▲▲ **Numbers involved**

Whole class.

———————— **What to do** ————————

Distribute the worksheet. Ask the children to draw pictures for each category specified on the worksheet. Explain that their work will be displayed and will be used for others to identify which drawing belongs to which person.

This is a 'finishing off' activity where the worksheets are available for individuals to do at an appropriate time.

When the sheets are displayed, place a piece of paper underneath each one, so that children can write who they think it is.

13 Who am I?

As an animal I would be . . .

As a colour I would be . . .

As a bird I would be . . .

As a flower I would be . . .

As a toy I would be . . .

As a musical instrument I would be . . .

14 ABC of personal qualities

Ⓟ Purpose

To help children to focus on how we differ from each other, other than in physical ways.

To develop alphabetical skills.

To illustrate personal qualities in humorous and creative ways.

To learn about using adjectives.

> Suggested age range

6+

⫽ Materials needed

Felt-tipped pens, pieces of paper for display, Blu-tak, alphabet chart or letters, pieces of card.

◗ Approximate timing

Adaptable to several sessions, at the teacher's discretion.

▶ What else it relates to

Who am I?

My personal coat of arms

Different parts of me

Qualities I look for in people

Personal tags

▲▲ Numbers involved

Whole class/small groups.

What to do

The class is invited to brainstorm words which describe people's personal qualities, e.g. funny, keen, polite, brave, cheerful.

Next, they are asked to line up according to the first letter of their first names – Andrew, Barinder, etc. Then the children are grouped so that, for instance, the A's, B's and C's form one group, the D's, E's and F's another, etc. Each group copies down those words from the brainstorm beginning with their letters, and puts each word on to a separate piece of paper.

The groups discuss what they mean by each word and then feed back to the whole group. Words can be checked in a dictionary if necessary. Older children may like to use a thesaurus to come up with alternatives to share with the rest of the class.

Using the alphabet chart, which many primary classes will already have around the room, the children are then invited to get up in turn and to put the words under or next to the corresponding big letter. This is a good activity to do at the end of a lesson and before a break.

The next step is to make an alphabet chart (if the class does not already have one) or a concertina book, illustrating some of the personal qualities already thought of but now linked to names of children in the class, e.g. Brave Brian, Energetic Emily. This can be done in a variety of ways, whether individually or in small groups, but the teacher must co-ordinate activities so that letters are not missed or duplicated.

15 My personal coat of arms

Ⓟ Purpose

To enhance self-confidence.
To provide an opportunity for self-reflection.

＞ Suggested age range

Any age.

✐ Materials needed

Photocopy of coat of arms for each participant (see p.70–71)

◕ Approximate timing

30 minutes.

▶ What else it relates to

Who am I?
ABC of personal qualities
A collage of me

👥 Numbers involved

Whole class.

What to do

The teacher distributes the coat of arms to each participant and then brainstorms, or suggests, a list of the categories that might be illustrated on them. The teacher explains that the point of this is to generate a list of ideas which can be drawn on the coat of arms, to inform other people about each participant: for instance, 'The most important things that have happened to me', 'The things I am good at', 'The things that make me happy', 'Words that describe me'.

The children then draw their personal image on each coat of arms and these are displayed around the classroom.

15 My personal coat of arms

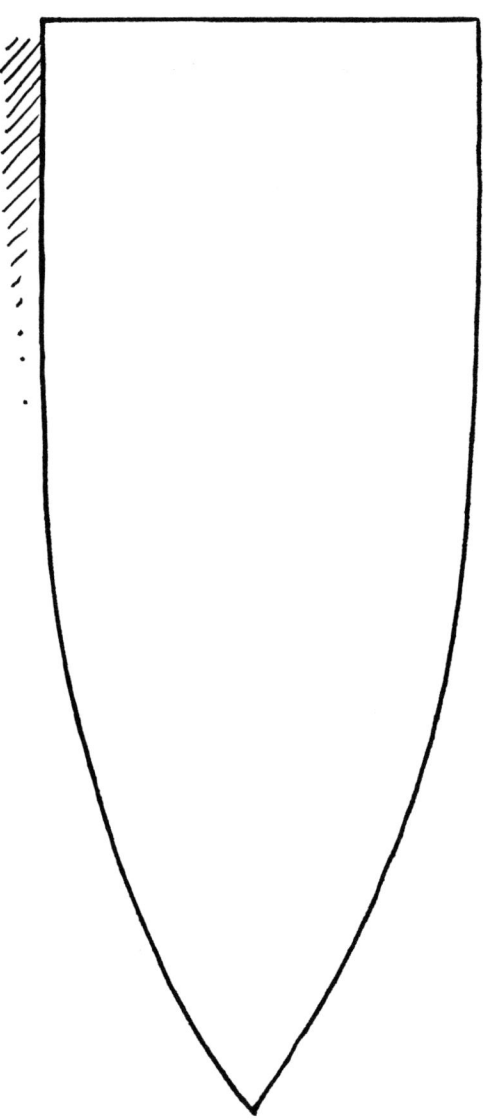

15 My personal coat of arms

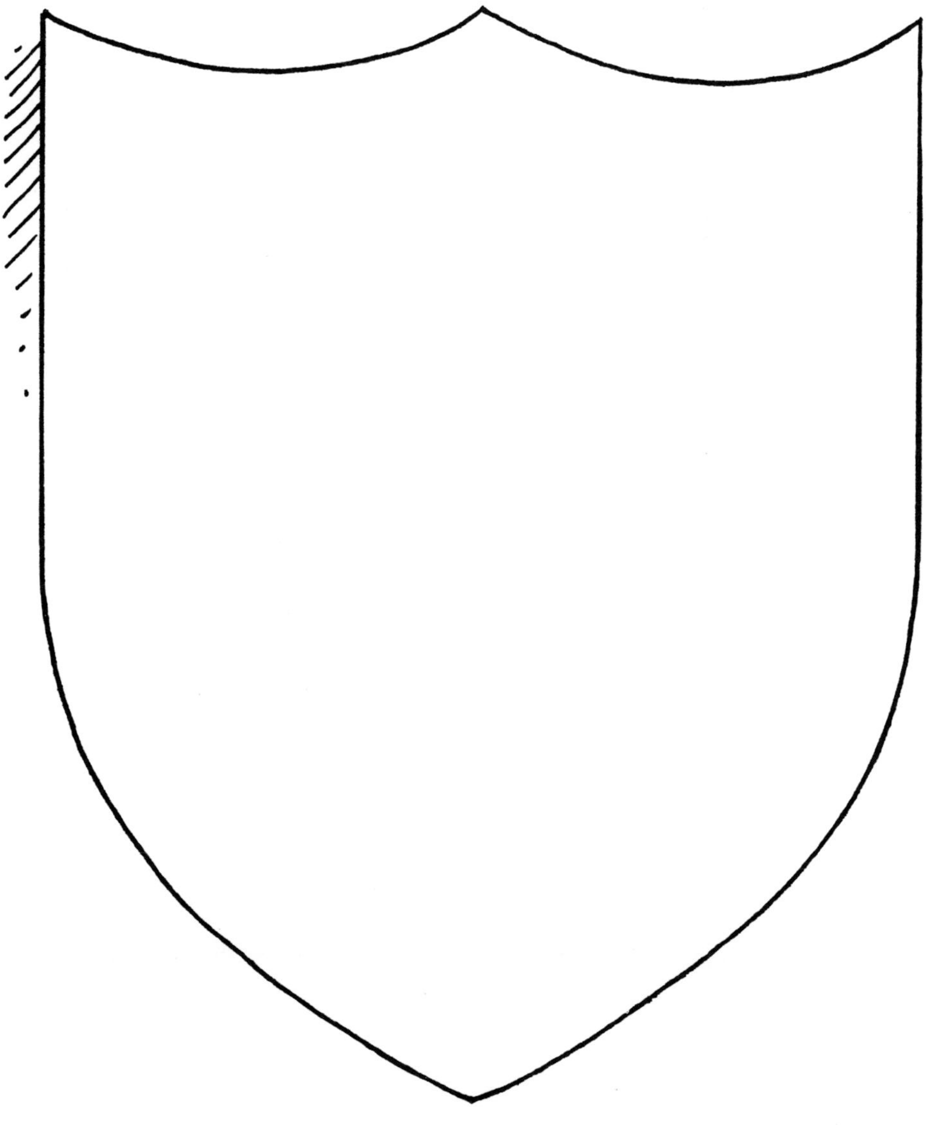

16 A collage of me

Ⓟ **Purpose**

To enhance a sense of self-identity.
To encourage children to respect personal differences.

〉 **Suggested age range**

Any age.

✍ **Materials needed**

Magazines, scissors, glue, paper.

◕ **Approximate timing**

30 minutes +

▶ **What else it relates to**

Who am I?
My personal coat of arms

👥 **Numbers involved**

Whole class.

What to do

The teacher introduces the session by encouraging a conversation about ways in which we are different. This can be done in pairs or threes. (You may wish to use an idea from Chapter 3 to group the children.)

The groups are asked to talk about their favourite foods, sports, subjects at school, hopes for the future, etc. These questions can either be 'fed in' by the teacher or generated by the children. It is a good idea to have them listed as an agenda to talk by.

The magazines, glue and scissors are then distributed. The children help each other to design posters which reflect their lives, using images from the magazines.

Each group then presents their pictures to the rest of the class.

17 Different parts of me

℗ Purpose

To consider how we are perceived by other people.

＞ Suggested age range

6+

∥ Materials needed

Large piece of paper and pencils or felt-tipped pens for each child.

◗ Approximate timing

25 minutes.

▶ What else it relates to

Who am I?
The ABC of personal qualities
Personal tags

👥 Numbers involved

Whole class.

What to do

The teacher asks the children to help to make a list of people and pets who are important to them. This can be done as a brainstorm.

The teacher then asks the children to divide their paper into four parts and explains that each child is to draw a self-portrait in the middle of the page.

Each child then selects four different people, or maybe a pet, who know her/him well, and is asked to illustrate, in each corner of the paper, the way in which each person perceives her/him. S/he can write underneath: 'As seen by . . .'.

This may well need to be preceded by a discussion about ways in which people see us differently. It is a good opportunity for teachers to bring a part of their personal history to the session.

The children can be encouraged to take their work home to find out if the people whom they have chosen agree with their perceptions.

18 We're all different

Ⓟ Purpose

To identify the ways in which we differ physically from each other. To appreciate that variety is an essential part of life.

> Suggested age range

Any age.

✏ Materials needed

Paper, pens, pencils, art materials.

◕ Approximate timing

30 minutes +

▶ What else it relates to

Work in Chapter 6 on parts of the body.

▲▲ Numbers involved

Whole class/small groups.

What to do

Depending on the age of the children, the teacher might want to explain how physical characteristics are inherited from parents and passed on in genes, which are brought together when the egg and sperm meet. Although brothers and sisters are often alike, each individual is totally unique – even identical twins!

The class is invited to brainstorm ways in which people are physically different, e.g. colour of eyes, height, hair colour, foot size, skin colour, weight, type of hair.

It is imperative in this kind of activity that the teacher is sensitive to anything likely to cause embarrassment or difficulties within the class. An example of this might be weight. Plump or fat children are sometimes picked on and called names; this activity could serve to draw attention to other children's thoughtless behaviour in this respect. The sensitive teacher will use this, if it arises, to raise awareness of the need to be sensitive to other people's feelings. Similarly, with colour of skin, the teacher must be aware of comments about racial differences which may be made. In schools with a multi-ethnic population, the school should be addressing this important aspect of life throughout the curriculum, and through the way in which the school is run.

When the brainstorm is finished, the class is divided into groups of three or four. Each group then gathers information on a particular topic (e.g. eye colour) from the entire class, and works out a way of presenting their data to the rest of the class. This could be in the form of bar charts, checklists, graphs, etc.

When each group has presented their information, the class decides who should present all of it together. This could be in the form of a wall display, class book, or a 'radio report' on tape.

19 Qualities I look for in people

Ⓟ Purpose

To encourage children to identify and appreciate the qualities that people have and to identify what is important to them.
To teach about adjectives and alliteration.
To practise alphabetical skills.

＞ Suggested age range

Upper Juniors.

▶ What else it relates to

ABC of personal qualities

∥ Materials needed

Flipchart/chalkboard, paper and pen for each child.

▲▲ Numbers involved

Whole class.

◕ Approximate timing

30 minutes.

What to do

The teacher begins the session with a round in which each child is asked to give a 'handle' to her or his name, which begins with the same letter. This can be part of developing an understanding of alliteration: for instance, 'I'm Positive Pete', 'I'm Laughing Leonie'.

This can lead to a brainstorm, as a whole class, of adjectives which are positive and which describe people.

The children are then asked to list the brainstormed words in alphabetical order. Once this is done, the children are divided into pairs. One of their lists is cut up, so that each strip of paper has one word on it.

In their pairs, the children are asked to sort the words into an order, with the most positive at one end and the word that is the least positive at the other, with all the other words graded in between.

The session can be finished by another round, where the children use one of the positive words to describe how they are feeling.

---

20 Personal tags

℗ Purpose

To offer the children the opportunity to express positive statements to each other.

＞ Suggested age range

Upper Infants/Juniors.

✎ Materials needed

Large pieces of paper, art materials, mirrors.

◕ Approximate timing

30 minutes.

▶ What else it relates to

ABC of personal qualities
Different parts of me

👥 Numbers involved

Whole class.

What to do

Using the mirrors, the children are asked to produce portraits of themselves.

These are displayed on the wall, with a blank piece of paper under each one.

The teacher then explains that the children can write positive comments under the pictures for each person.

21 Plotting people

Ⓟ Purpose

To analyse relationships, both in general and in particular.
To generate adjectives to describe people.

⟩ Suggested age range

Juniors.

✏ Materials needed

Pieces of paper for each
pair, pens or pencils.
A 'symbols' display for
the whole class.

◑ Approximate timing

30 minutes.

▶ What else it relates to

Risk factor
How I keep myself safe
Who can I turn to?
Boys and girls go out to
play
Forces of persuasion

👥 Numbers involved

Whole class.

What to do

The teacher begins the session by talking about how we like and do not like different
people, and introduces symbols to indicate this. For example:

$A \rightarrow B$ = A likes B
$A \leftrightarrow B$ = Both A and B like each other
$A --> B$ = A does not like B
$A <--> B$ = A and B do not like each other
$A </\/\> B$ = A feels okay but has no really strong feelings about B

The class can invent their own symbols.

The children are divided into pairs. They are asked to talk about a favourite TV
programme and to produce a *sociogram* of the relationships between the characters.

This can lead to a discussion of why people do/do not get along. In pairs, the children
can produce adjectives which we use to describe other people. These adjectives can
be used in a piece of creative writing.

Individually, the children might produce a sociogram of people whom they like, and
label the people with adjectives which they could use to describe them.

This can lead into a discussion about people whom we can trust, and to whom we
can go if we need to talk about any situation.

22 What I need / What I want

ⓟ Purpose

To differentiate between needs and wants.
To show that everyone's needs and wants are different.

⟩ Suggested age range

7 – 11.

⫽ Materials needed

Plenty of sheets of drawing paper, red and green felt-tipped pens or coloured pencils/pens, Blu-tak, glue.

◕ Approximate timing

30 minutes +

▶ What else it relates to

Who am I?
Graphing out our needs and wants.
My ideal day

▲▲ Numbers involved

Whole class.

What to do

The children do drawings in red of 'Things I can't do without', e.g. food, bed, clothes, heat, friends. They then do drawings in green of 'Things I want but could do without', e.g. TV, bicycle, skateboard. They cut out each drawing.

The teacher gives out blank paper to each child. The children either write 'Me' or draw themselves in the centre of the sheet, then lay their drawings close to the centre or further away, according to how they feel about needing or wanting the items.

Working with the person next to them, the children compare their sheets.
The drawings can be moved if they wish, then are secured with Blu-tak.

The teacher can lead a discussion about the activity, asking:
  'Did you move many drawings?'

'Why/Why not?'
'Did you change your mind about anything?'
'What have you learned about needs/wants?'

The children use glue to make their drawings permanent. The sheets can be displayed around the classroom.

Variation: 'In someone else's shoes'

Before the drawings are stuck down, children are given another piece of paper. They select someone who is very different to themselves (e.g. of opposite sex, older, younger). They put this other person at the centre of the sheet, then place the drawings according to what they think that that person's needs and wants are.

They might then share what they have done with a partner, or the teacher could choose to ask:

'How did you decide what the other person's needs or wants are?'
'Do you think you are right?'
'Do you need to do more drawings?'
'Are people's needs and wants different?'
'Is this a good thing?'

The teacher may choose to debrief the activity either in the whole group or by breaking it down into smaller groups.

23 Graphing out our needs and wants

(P) **Purpose**

To identify needs and wants and to differentiate between them. To explore other people's values in terms of needs and wants.

> **Suggested age range**

9 – 11.

Materials needed

Coordinate grids previously made by children, pencils.

Approximate timing

20 minutes, excluding making the grids.

▶ **What else it relates to**

Who am I?
What I need/What I want
My ideal day

Numbers involved

Whole class.

What to do

After mathematical work on coordinates, the teacher asks the class to produce individual coordinate grids, with each axis going from 0 – 4.

When these have been completed, the teacher initiates a brainstorm and discussion on 'What do we all need/want?'. The teacher assigns a letter to each item produced in the brainstorm.

Each child selects six items which are most important in terms of needs. The teacher invites the children to place these items, using the code letter, on their coordinate grids. At this stage it is important that these are not shared with anyone else.

By using an idea from *ABC of workshop ideas*, Chapter 3, the children form pairs. One person is A, the other B. A begins by offering a coordinate (e.g. 3, 2). B has to say whether a letter is there or not. If a letter is on the coordinate offered, then A can ask three questions to identify what B has chosen as one of his/her needs on that coordinate. If A fails, then B has a turn, and the activity continues in this way.

Follow-up activities

Useful debrief questions might include:

'What do you think your needs/wants might be when you are fifteen?'
'What were they when you were three?'
'What do you think might be the needs/wants of a single parent with a toddler?'
'What do you think are the needs/wants of an elderly person living alone?'

The teacher might want to involve a small group of children in collecting all of the grids in order to produce a class bar chart showing the whole range of needs and wants. This could lead to further discussion and could also entail children exploring the needs and wants of other age ranges in the school and beyond.

24 My ideal day

Ⓟ Purpose

To identify our own wants and needs and to express what we feel.
To develop mathematical skills.
To promote discussion on similarities and differences between people.

＞ Suggested age range

All ages. Pie chart might be provided for younger age groups.

✏️ Materials needed

Compasses, paper, pencils, art materials, rulers.

◕ Approximate timing

At the discretion of the teacher.

▶ What else it relates to

Who am I?
What I need/What I want
Graphing out our needs and wants

♟ Numbers involved

Whole class.

——————— What to do ———————

This activity would be part of work being done on expressing data in a variety of ways. The teacher will have introduced the concept of pie charts, which involves drawing circles, and segmenting the circles into a number of parts. The teacher may then wish to divide the class into three or four groups. Each group may be given a different topic to talk about. For example:

'What is the worst day you have ever had?'
'What is an average day for your group?'
'Think of a really good day, perhaps in your holidays. Why do some days seem better than others?'

After feedback from each group, the teacher asks each of the children to produce a pie chart, divided into 24 hourly segments, which illustrates her/his perfect day. The class may then be divided into pairs to share their perfect days. During feedback, the teacher might want to identify similarities and differences. This can lead to exploration of gender, race and class issues.

Variations

The children might want to explore a perfect day for their carer or teacher, or try to predict what the perfect day of their brother or sister might be.

The children could attempt 'the perfect day' of a heroine or hero. This could lead to a discussion about fantasies and realities, and might form part of media studies work.

This may lead to creative writing activities, where the children create a character of their own.

25 Bar chart feelings graph

Ⓟ **Purpose**

To encourage children to reflect on their learning experiences.
To acknowledge the importance of feelings and how to express them.

\> **Suggested age range**

8 +

// **Materials needed**

Graph paper, pencils, rulers, coloured pencils.

◐ **Approximate timing**

5 minutes per use. Initial construction of the bar chart might be 20 – 30 minutes.

▶ **What else it relates to**

Feeling barometers
My personal feelings
Painting a feeling
The feelings collection
Circles of feelings

👥 **Numbers involved**

Individual activity within the whole class.

What to do

The teacher allows time for each child to construct a graph with feelings ratings as the vertical axis, and time measurements (days of the week, perhaps divided into mornings and afternoons) on the horizontal axis.

Once the graph is made, it can be used at the appropriate times to illustrate how each child is feeling about her/his own learning. The children would mark in a bar line to indicate this.

The bar charts can be used to 'trigger' discussions in pairs, small groups, or as a whole class.

26 Feeling barometers

Ⓟ **Purpose**

To allow children to express their feelings at any specific time.

> **Suggested age range**

All ages.

✏ **Materials needed**

Lollipop sticks, card, pencils/paints or felt-tipped pens, Blu-tak.

◕ **Approximate timing**

15 minutes.

▶ **What else it relates to**

Bar chart feelings graph
My personal feelings log
Painting a feeling.
The feelings collection
Circles of feelings

👥 **Numbers involved**

Whole class.

What to do

The teacher initiates discussion about how faces can express feelings. This can be made into a miming game. For instance, the teacher might say, 'Show me a happy face/ sad face'. Gradations of feeling may be introduced, along with new vocabulary, e.g. 'This is a threatening face. What do you think threatening means?'

The children are then asked to draw two faces, one happy and one sad, on small pieces of card. They attach each of these to the end of a lollipop stick. The blu-tak is used to allow the lollipop stick to stand up.

The faces can be used on the children's tables so that the children can signal how they are feeling at any particular time which may be chosen by the teacher.

Variation

A more sophisticated version would be to encourage the children to calibrate a long strip of thick card. They could write feelings words, starting with very happy at one end of the card to extremely sad at the other. They might use these to indicate how they are feeling at any given moment. They can do this by pointing or by using coloured dots attached to blu-tak.

27 My personal feelings log

(P) **Purpose**

To encourage children to analyse events and situations which make them feel good or bad.
To recognise that individuals respond differently.

> **Suggested age range**

Upper Infants and Juniors.

✏ **Materials needed**

Photocopies of worksheet on p. 87, large sheets of paper, felt-tipped pens.

◑ **Approximate timing**

At the discretion of the teacher or child.

▶ **What else it relates to**

Bar chart feelings graph
Feeling barometers
Painting a feeling
The feelings collection
Circles of feelings

👥 **Numbers involved**

Small groups; individuals with worksheet.

What to do

The teacher should make sure that the children are aware that we respond and feel differently towards different things. This awareness may be achieved through some of the work activities in this book.

The teacher divides the class into groups of three/four and gives each group a large sheet of paper. The children draw a line down the middle of the page. On one side of the line, they make lists of things that make them feel good; things that make them feel bad are listed on the other side. This can lead to a whole class discussion.

Having distributed the worksheet, the teacher explains that each child is going to be able to keep a personal log of things that make them feel good or bad over a period of time. The children can elect to fill out the logs at certain times or this can be directed by the teacher.

From time to time, the children can be encouraged to share their responses and feed back to the whole class.

27 My personal feelings log

MY NAME IS ....

I AM STARTING THIS LOG ON ....

	🙂	🙁
MONDAY		
TUESDAY		
WEDNESDAY		
THURSDAY		
FRIDAY		

We all feel differently about different things. Fill out your personal log each day. Write down the things that make you feel good or bad. Share your ideas with a partner.

28 Painting a feeling

Ⓟ **Purpose**

To show that feelings can be expressed in different ways.
Music appreciation.
Developing art skills/listening skills.
To promote discussion about differences and similarities between people.

> **Suggested age range**

All ages.

✐ **Materials needed**

Music, art materials.

◖ **Approximate timing**

At the discretion of the teacher.

▶ **What else it relates to**

Bar chart feelings graph
Feeling barometers
My personal feelings log
The feelings collection
Circles of feelings

👥 **Numbers involved**

Small groups.

———— What to do ————

The teacher introduces a discussion on how music can express feelings and plays a variety of examples. For instance, lullabies are calm, panpipes may sound sad, marches evoke feelings of bravery. This activity can be used as a movement lesson.

Having distributed art materials, the teacher might invite the children to listen to the music, take up brushes/crayons and paint their feelings.

The paintings can be used to stimulate a class discussion.

The paintings may also be displayed with a sign saying, 'Gives the feelings of . . .'. Blank paper can be put up under the paintings for children to write their ideas.

29 The feelings collection

℗ Purpose

To acknowledge the feelings that we have, both positive and negative.

To introduce new vocabulary.

To encourage children to reflect on their feelings.

> Suggested age range

Any age.

∅ Materials needed

Large sheet of paper on the wall with some 'feeling' words (see reference list on p.91). This is intended as a permanent display, and the class can add to the list.

◑ Approximate timing

At the discretion of the teacher.

▶ What else it relates to

Bar chart feelings graph
Feeling barometers
My personal feelings log
Painting a feeling
Circles of feelings
Attraction reaction
Reading our feelings

▲▲ Numbers involved

Small groups, to whole class.

What to do

The teacher introduces the words on the feeling list by saying, 'I feel . . . when I . . .'.

The children take turns to choose a word from the list and to make up a sentence beginning, 'I feel . . . when I . . .'. This can be spoken at first, and then written down. The teacher can encourage children to add new words.

This growing list can be used at any time during the school day. The teacher might choose to stop a group activity and ask:

'How are you feeling at the moment? Choose a word from the list.'
'Why are you feeling this way?'
'Can you think of a new feeling word to add to the list?'

Variations

Once the long list has been established, older children will be able to sort the feelings words into a personal order, grouping words according to whether they are comfortable or uncomfortable feelings. To facilitate this, teachers might choose to use the idea of a diagram, such as the examples below:

THINGS THAT MAKE ME				
ANGRY	SAD	HAPPY	FRUSTRATED	etc.

This can lead to discussions amongst children (grouping activities are given in Chapter 3):

'Do we all react in the same way?'
'Will the diagram always look like this?'
'Can you group the uncomfortable feelings in any way?'
'What can you do about feelings of anger, etc.?'

29 The feelings collection

anxious	frightened	puzzled
apologetic	frustrated	
		relieved
bashful	happy	
bored	horrified	sad
	hot	shocked
cold	hurt	surprised
concentrating		
confident	indifferent	thoughtful
curious	interested	
		undecided
determined	lonely	
disappointed	lovestruck	
disgusted		
	mischevious	
envious	miserable	
exasperated		
exhausted	negative	

30 Circles of feelings

People often use phrases to explain their feelings. Here is a list of some of those phrases:

> On top of the world.
> Swallowed up.
> Wanting the floor to open up.
> Down in the dumps.
> It's the pits.
> Over the moon.
> Sick as a parrot.
> Feeling down.
> Getting a kick out of something.
> In a corner.
> Jumping for joy.

Add more to the list if you can.

Now make up your own pictures to go with each of these 'phrases'. Do you know what they all mean?

Try this out with someone at home.

Come up with a new expression of your own, and design a picture of it.

31 Risk factor

Ⓟ **Purpose**

To show that we all have different perceptions of risk.
To identify risky situations, and strategies to handle them.

〉 **Suggested age range**

9 – 11.

✏ **Materials needed**

Photocopy of 'Dangerous things' (p. 95), cut up for each group.
Large sheet of paper, felt-tipped pens, and Blu-tak for each group.

◕ **Approximate timing**

30 minutes.

▶ **What else it relates to**

Plotting people
How I keep myself safe
Forces of persuasion

👥 **Numbers involved**

Small groups.

What to do

The teacher forms groups of 4–5 children, using one of the ideas from Chapter 3, and distributes one pack of 'Dangerous things' cards to each group, asking them to place them face down.

Each group is given a large sheet of paper and asked to draw a line on it, with zero at one end and 10 at the other.

The teacher explains that zero indicates 'no risk' and that 10 is 'very high risk indeed'. (At this point, the teacher may choose to take suggestions from the class about what kind of thing may be near zero and what might be near 10.)

The teacher then explains that this is a guessing game and that the child whose turn it is must try to predict where the unseen card, face down at the top of the pile, might be placed on the line.

The first child predicts, then reveals the card. As a group, the children must decide where to place the card on the 0–10 continuum. Once they have agreed, the danger card is fixed in the appropriate position. The children take it in turns to work through the pack of cards.

At a given moment, the children are asked to join with another group to compare where they have placed the cards. The teacher may then wish to offer questions to enhance the learning. For example:

> 'Did you agree?'
> 'What did you disagree about?'
> 'What risks did you think about?'
> 'What can you do for yourselves about the risks?'

As a final activity, the whole class could brainstorm what they have learned about risk-taking.

Variations and extensions

The children can be encouraged to devise their own 'risk' cards.

They can produce creative writing.

They can watch the *Good Health* video (see Resource list in Chapter 7).

31 Risk factor: dangerous things

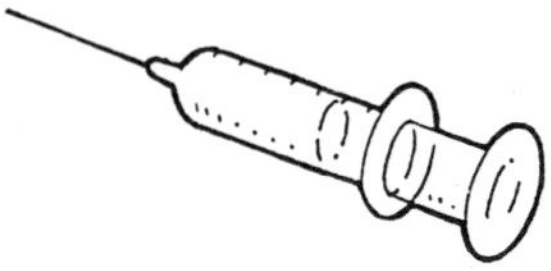

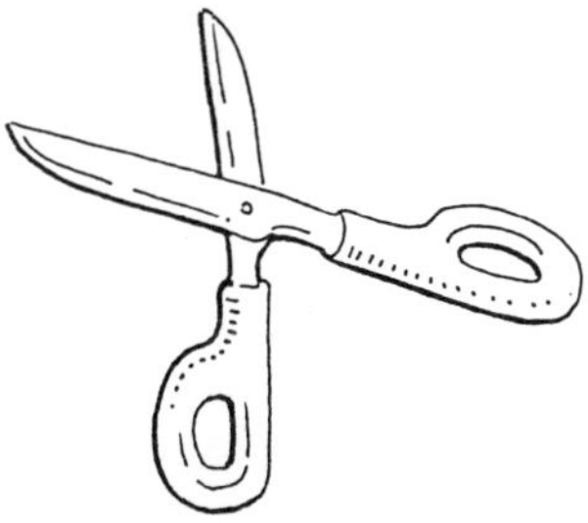

32 How I keep myself safe

Ⓟ **Purpose**

To develop a concept of safety in relationship to others.
To develop an understanding of how safety is ensured.

> **Suggested age range**

7 – 11.

✍ **Materials needed**

Large sheets of paper, felt-tipped pens.

◕ **Approximate timing**

30 minutes.

▶ **What else it relates to**

Plotting people
Risk factor
Forces of persuasion

👥 **Numbers involved**

Whole class.

What to do

The teacher leads a general discussion or brainstorm on 'Things that need to be kept safe', e.g. pets, babies, old people, precious objects, etc.

Using any of the ideas from Chapter 3, the teacher divides the class into groups of four/five. Large sheets of paper and felt-tipped pens are given to each group. The children list ways in which things are kept safe, e.g. obedience training for pets, playpens for babies, variety of safety aids for old people, traffic lights, etc.

The teacher asks each group to pass on their list to the next group. Each child in that group takes it in turn to mime one way in which things are kept safe. The other children have to guess which one it is.

Variation

Instead of using a large sheet of paper, small pieces of card could be used to list each idea and the cards could be passed on face down.

33 Who can I turn to?

ⓟ **Purpose**

To identify significant people in our lives whom we can trust.
To celebrate this trust.

> **Suggested age range**

Any age.

✏ **Materials needed**

Paper, art materials.

◐ **Approximate timing**

30 minutes.

▶ **What else it relates to**

Plotting people.

👥 **Numbers involved**

Whole class.

What to do

The teacher uses the 'Plotting people' activity (p.77) to begin a discussion on trust.

The children are asked to list all of the people whom they trust and to draw pictures of them. These can be produced as a booklet. Alternatively, the children might select one of the people to make a 'Thank you' card for.

34 I enjoy being . . .

Ⓟ **Purpose**

To investigate stereotyping.

> **Suggested age range**

Upper Juniors.

✏ **Materials needed**

Photocopies of questionnaire on p.100, large pieces of paper, scissors, pens.

◔ **Approximate timing**

30 minutes.

▶ **What else it relates to**

ABC of jobs
Sherlock Holmes
Picture triggers

👥 **Numbers involved**

Whole class working individually, then in small groups.

———————— # What to do ————————

The teacher distributes the questionnaire and allows time for the children to fill it out.

The children are formed into small groups (using an idea from Chapter 3). In groups the children are asked to draw large circles, as below:

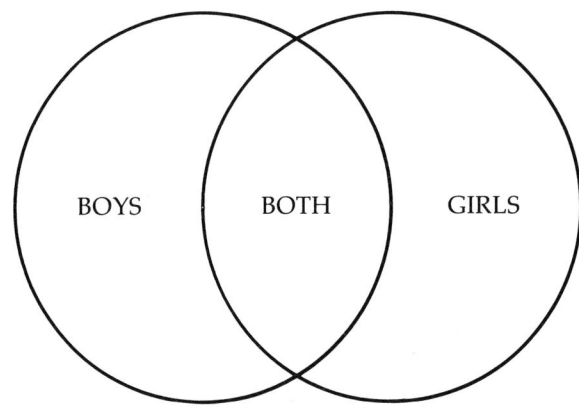

They then cut up their questionnaires so that each statement is on a separate piece of paper. They place these 'reply strips' face down in the middle of the group. The children take it in turns to select one of the statements and to place it where they think it belongs within the circles.

The teacher encourages the children to discuss each placing and to negotiate as a group if it is appropriate.

At the end of the activity, the teacher asks the children:

'Did you all agree?'
'What caused the most talk?'
'What have you learned about boys' and girls' ideas?'
'Was anyone surprised about where your own reply strips were placed?'
'What have you learned by doing this activity?'

34 I enjoy being . . .

Questionnaire

I enjoy being a girl/boy because . . .

1. ....

2. ....

3. ....

4. ....

5. ....

6. ....

I don't like being a girl/boy because . . .

1. ....

2. ....

3. ....

4. ....

5. ....

6. ....

The toys and games I like to play with are . . .

1. ....

2. ....

3. ....

4. ....

5. ....

6. ....

35 ABC of jobs

Ⓟ **Purpose**

To encourage the children to recognise that jobs are not the perogative of any particular gender.
To practise alphabetical skills.
To produce an alphabet book.

> **Suggested age range**

Any Junior class.

✏️ **Materials needed**

Paper, art materials, felt-tipped pens.

◕ **Approximate timing**

Initial session approx. 30 minutes. Continuing project thereafter.

▶ **What else it relates to**

I enjoy being . . .
Sherlock Holmes
Picture triggers

👥 **Numbers involved**

Whole class.

What to do

The teacher divides the class into four groups (using ideas from Chapter 3 to do this).

Two of the groups are asked to list traditionally 'male' jobs and an ABC of male names on separate sheets of paper. The other two groups make a list of 'female' jobs and an ABC of female names on separate sheets of paper.

When they have done this, the teacher asks the groups to exchange the lists of names, so that the 'male' job groups have female names, and vice versa.

The groups then produce an alphabet book of jobs and names, using the names that they have been given. The teacher may need to give an example of this, e.g. Daniel the Dinner Helper or Sarah the Scaffolder.

Once the books have been made, they can be displayed in the classroom, and given to other classes.

36 Boys and girls go out to play

℗ Purpose

To analyse playground games and how much space boys and girls use.

> Suggested age range

Upper juniors.

✍ Materials needed

Worksheet on pp. 103–104.

◕ Approximate timing

Variable according to child/teacher interest.

▶ What else it relates to

Plotting people
I enjoy being . . .
The ABC of jobs
Sherlock Holmes
Picture triggers

👥 Numbers involved

Small groups.

―――――― What to do ――――――

The teacher may choose to use all or part of the worksheet. The children will need to have the tasks on the worksheet explained/clarified.

36 Boys and girls go out to play

In your groups, list all of the games that go on in the playground. You may want to ask younger or older children in your school. Check out your list with others.

Over several playtimes, watch what games are being played. Use the code B (for Boys) G (for Girls) and write down who plays what.

Present your report to the rest of the class.
Ask them questions like:

'Do boys and girls get a fair share of the playground?'
'If not, why not?'
'What can be done about it?'

You may want to do a more in-depth study.
Draw a rough plan of the shape of the playground.
When you are watching what is going on at playtimes, put the letter B on your plan where the boys use the playground and the letter G where the girls use it.
You might need to do this over several playtimes.

Is it fair?
If not, what can be done about it?

Show the results to the rest of the class. Ask them if they agree with your findings and your ideas.

Plan your ideal playground.
When you have done this, share your plan with others.
Ask them if they like it. Explain why you have made it in the way that you have.

Does it meet the needs of everybody?
What would others change about your design?

Do a survey of likes and dislikes about your playground.
Do you need to talk about the actual games played?

37 Sherlock Holmes

℗ Purpose

To encourage children to explore their views of others.
To challenge stereotyping.

⟩ Suggested age range

Upper Juniors.

✎ Materials needed

Four carrier bags, each containing four different items of clothing. (A wider selection of clothes will lead to a more interesting discussion.)

🕐 Approximate timing

One hour for group work; 30 minutes for follow-up discussion.

▶ What else it relates to

I enjoy being . . .
ABC of jobs
Picture triggers

👥 Numbers involved

Whole class divided into four groups.

What to do

The class is divided into four groups. (Use an idea from Chapter 3 to do this.)

Each group is given a bag of clothes. On a given signal, the children open the bag. They are given thirty minutes to discuss the type of person who might wear the clothes, to produce a drawing of what that person might look like, and to write a short piece about their person.

After thirty minutes, each group passes on the bag to another group. The process is repeated.

As a follow-up to this activity, the teacher leads a discussion to compare the various outcomes. The pictures and pieces of writing should be on display.

Questions to help the process might include:

'Did we all think the same way?'
'If yes, why? If no, why not?'
'Can we tell what a person is like from what they wear?'
'How can we tell what people are like?'

A statement such as 'Even when we think we know people well, they may do something unexpected' can lead to further discussions with the class.

---

38 Picture triggers

Ⓟ Purpose

To explore assumptions and variations in lifestyles.

＞ Suggested age range

Upper Juniors.

✏ Materials needed

Photocopies of each set of picture triggers and statements for each group (see pp. 107–108), blank cards, art materials.

◕ Approximate timing

30 minutes +

▶ Numbers involved

Whole class.

♟ What else it relates to

Risk factor
I enjoy being
The ABC of who
Sherlock Holmes

What to do

The teacher divides the class into pairs and distributes the sets of cards, which have been cut up earlier.

The teacher asks each group to place the pictures in a line and then to decide which of the statement cards should be placed beneath each picture. The children may be offered the opportunity to write their own statements on blank sheets of card.

The teacher then asks the children to form groups of four to compare responses. They must try to reach agreement on their 'match-ups'. This can lead to a discussion by the whole class of stereotypes.

Following this, there may be a discussion about the variety of lifestyles that people choose. Afterwards, the teacher may wish to distribute blank cards and to ask the children to draw pictures of the type of lifestyle that each pictured character will have in ten years' time.

This might lead to a guessing game, where only the children's drawings are displayed, and the class is given the opportunity to identify which drawing goes with which original picture. Here is an opportunity to continue discussion about stereotypes and lifestyle variations.

As a development to the session, any of the pictures may be used as a stimulus for creative writing.

38 Picture triggers

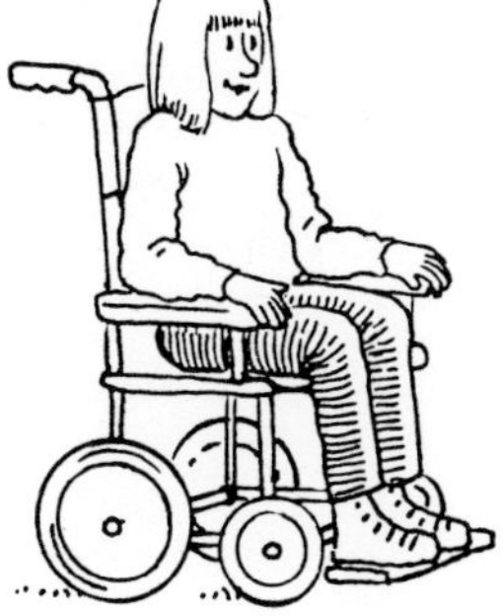

38 Picture triggers: suggested statements

I don't like relying on other people.	I think looks are very important.	I don't care what other people think about me.
Most people around here seem selfish.	You have to look like this to survive.	I think it is important that parents are strict with children.
Friendships are really important.	How people speak is important.	Looking after other people is important.

·5·
Nothing
stays the same

Much of the work in this section will involve knowledge which may be beyond the children's experiences, and so there will be a place for some direct teaching. To support this, we are offering ideas which will:

- Encourage children to be actively involved in their own learning.
- Offer strategies to assess children's understanding.
- Develop ideas for the children to explore their values and attitudes.
- Offer ways of acknowledging that much of the content is concerned with feelings.
- Give factual information for children. Some of the pages in this section are merely *example* factsheets, as this is not a sex education manual. We do offer some factual information for teachers. The Resource list in Chapter 7 will be helpful.

In considering this work, we remind you of the need:

- To check out guidelines for your school/LEA.
- To check out how the parents are involved/informed.
- To be aware of your own attitudes/values and of how these might be transmitted.

39 Words, words, words

℗ Purpose

To encourage children to think about the language that they use.

> Suggested age range

Upper Juniors.

✐ Materials needed

Large sheets of paper, pens/pencils, photocopies of worksheet on p.112. Copies of the anatomical drawings on pp. 128–129 might be useful.

◕ Approximate timing

30 minutes.

▶ What else it relates to

Suggestion box
Questions in a hat

▲▲ Numbers involved

Whole class (in pairs).

What to do

The teacher may wish to begin this session by discussing how we use words to suit the group whom we are addressing. For example, we would not say 'Coochie Coochie' to the headteacher.

The teacher then explains that the worksheet is asking the children to think of polite ways of expressing ideas. There may be a need to use the anatomical drawings to help the children to be aware of the medical words for body parts.

The teacher may wish to offer the children the opportunity to write down any concerns that they have about language, which can be posted in the class suggestion box (see p.155).

39 Words, words, words

Polite ───────────────────────── Impolite

Find a partner.
Draw a line like the one above at the top of a sheet of paper.

Think of how you feel sometimes and the words that you use.
For example, you might want to be alone.
Think of what you might say that is not polite. You do not have to write this down.
Now turn it into a polite word or phrase.
Write down the polite form.

Try this out with these ideas:

- You want to go to the toilet.
- You need to tell an adult that someone has sworn at you.
- You want to describe the sexual body parts of a man.
- You want to describe the sexual body parts of a woman.
- You want to describe a sexual activity.

Can you think of any others?
Write down polite ways of saying them.

40 I can understand you

Ⓟ Purpose

To help the children to pronounce and understand medical words. To produce a 'medical wordbook'.

> Suggested age range

Upper Juniors.

✎ Materials needed

Photocopies of worksheet on p.114, chalkboard and chalk or large sheets of paper and felt-tipped pens for each group.

◐ Approximate timing

30 minutes.

▶ What else it relates to

Any new words which are introduced to the children.

▲▲ Numbers involved

Whole class.

What to do

The teacher should explain that there are all kinds of words that are used which children might have difficulty in saying and understanding.

Having offered the children a list of these words, the teacher should then explain that they are going to make pictograms of them.

First, however, the class is divided into groups. Each group is given a copy of the worksheet. They are asked to work out the words from the pictures. After a given time, the words are shared. At this stage, the children may be encouraged to devise their own codes for the medical words that they need to know.

40 I can understand you

Can you work out the words from the pictures?

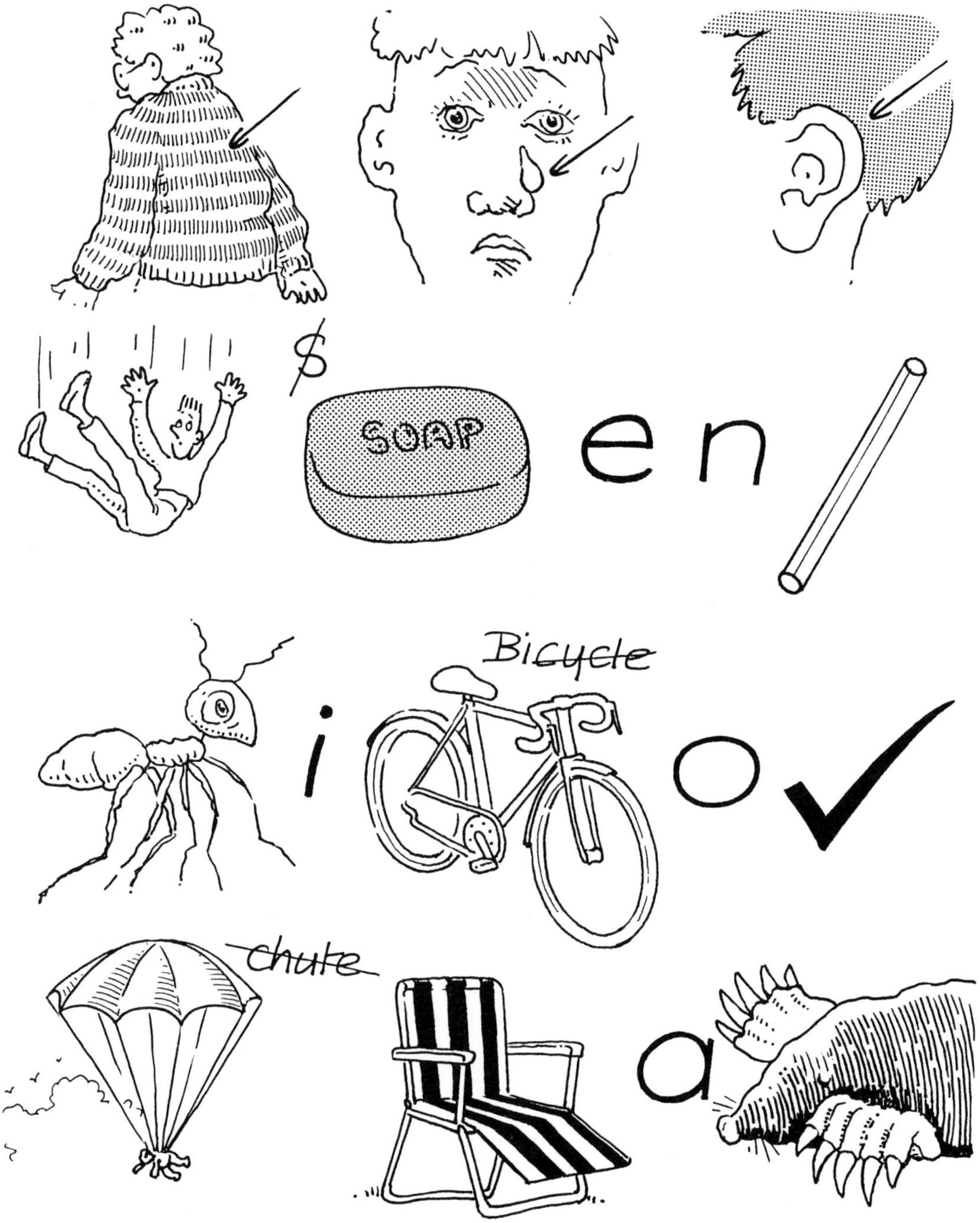

SOAP

e n

Bicycle

i O ✓

chute

a

41 Body talk

Ⓟ Purpose

To identify different anatomical parts, and to elicit from the children which areas of the body are private.

> Suggested age range

Upper Juniors.

∦ Materials needed

Photocopies of male/female bodies (see pp. 124–125), blank paper, art materials.

◕ Approximate timing

30 minutes.

▶ What else it relates to

Naming the frame
Fishing for facts
Female or male?
Forces of persuasion
Checking out the facts

▲▲ Numbers involved

Whole class.

_____ # What to do _____

The teacher distributes blank paper and asks the children to draw an outline of their own body and to mark in the correct position as many words to do with the body as possible.

The children form pairs to compare their body outlines and words. The teacher then distributes the appropriate body picture (male or female) and asks the children to add to their own outline words that they have missed out.

Then the children are given the opportunity to colour in their outlines in different colours to indicate which parts of the body that they like/do not like being touched. These pictures can be collected in providing information for the teacher.

At a later stage, this information can be used by the teacher to lead a discussion about personal space and our right to our own bodies.

42 Naming the frame

ⓟ **Purpose**

To identify different body parts.

To assist the teacher in finding out children's knowledge and attitudes.

> **Suggested age range**

Older Juniors.

✐ **Materials needed**

Photocopies of male/female bodies (see pp. 124–125) cut up into parts.

◕ **Approximate timing**

30 minutes.

▶ **What else it relates to**

Body talk

Fishing for facts

Female or male?

Suggestion box

Questions in a hat

Checking out the facts

👥 **Numbers involved**

Whole class.

What to do

The teacher divides the class into pairs and distributes the fragmented drawing of the body to each pair (some will be male and some female). The children are asked to piece together the body and to name at least 15 parts. (To facilitate this, the teacher may choose to do a whole class brainstorm of parts of the body.)

Having named at least 15 parts, the children can be asked to place individual pieces of the body in a line according to the criterion most useful for the teacher. This might be, for instance, 'parts you know about to parts you know very little about' or perhaps 'parts you find embarrassing to those you do not find embarrassing.'

T

Variation

The children should be given one copy of the whole page and asked to name 15 parts of the body on their own and without showing anyone else.

They can then be asked to put a number alongside ten of the parts that they have named.

The class is divided into pairs and the pairs labelled A and B. The pairs are not allowed to show each other their pieces of paper. Instead, A goes first and names a part of the body. If B has a number against that part, A scores the appropriate amount of points for that part; if not, then no points are scored. Then it is B's turn to name a body part. The game continues in this fashion, until stopped by the teacher.

43 Fishing for facts

Ⓟ Purpose

To identify parts of the body.
To assist in learning how to spell words to do with the body.
To encourage collaborative learning.

> Suggested age range

In this form, upper Infants and lower Juniors.

✏ Materials needed

Magnets attached to lengths of string, paper shapes of body parts (see pp. 124–125 for diagrams) with paper clips attached, container, cards with the names of the body parts.

◕ Approximate timing

20 minutes.

▶ What else it relates to

Body talk
Naming the frame
Female or male?
Checking out the facts
Getting organised

👥 Numbers involved

Small groups.

What to do

The teacher forms the class into groups of four. Each group has several cards with names of parts of the body written on them, and paper-clipped shapes corresponding to each of these body parts.

The cards are placed face down in the middle of the group, and the shapes are put into a container. Each child takes one card, and then they each take it in turns to 'fish' for the part of the body named on their card.

If the child fishes out the correct part, s/he keeps it. If not, it is put back into the container. Alternatively, if the child who has fished out a shape sees that another child has the name of that part on their card, s/he can give the body part to the other child, providing that the child can spell the name of that part without looking at his or her card.

This continues until all of the parts of the body have been fished out. Then the children attempt to piece together the different shapes to make a whole body.

Variations

As the children become familiar with more complex parts of the body, these of course can be used.

It is also a useful activity to deal with terminology to do with sexual organs. A more sophisticated version might take the class into an understanding of the internal workings of the body. This can be done by means of a transparency which has on it the outer body shape.

44 Getting organised

Ⓟ **Purpose**

To identify the name, shape and function of internal body organs. To identify where these are in the body.

\> **Suggested age range**

Adaptable for every age range.

✐ **Materials needed**

Outlines of both the body and major organs (see pp. 124–127 for diagrams) enlarged to A3 size on a photocopier, Blu-tak, large sheets of paper, felt-tipped pens.

◑ **Approximate timing**

30 minutes +.

▶ **What else it relates to**

Fishing for facts
Female or male?
Checking out the facts

👥 **Numbers involved**

Whole class.

What to do

Before beginning this exercise, the teacher must number each set of organs 1, 2 or 3. These are then distributed to the class. The children try to find others with the same organ and, as a group, decide what function it performs.

The children record their ideas on a large sheet of paper and share these with the rest of the class. This leads to a whole class discussion. The teacher at this point can correct any errors which the children make.

The children reform into three groups, according to the number on each organ, and assemble the organs on the body outlines, using Blu-tak. They then label each organ with its name and function.

The whole class is invited to look at each completed outline and to comment.

Variation

This activity can be carried out in a large hall. The pictures and/or names of the organs can be placed at different points around the room. The teacher asks the group to sit in the middle of the hall and explains that they are going to participate in an activity similar to 'Port and Starboard'.

Instead of shouting 'port' or 'starboard', the teacher will call out the name of a particular organ. The children have to run towards where the picture or image of that organ is placed in the room. Alternatively, the teacher might want to describe what that organ does. Here again the children have to go in the direction of the organ which fits the description.

As in 'Port and Starboard', some instructions will be devised to encourage children *not* to move to a particular part of the room. These activities can be introduced by the words: 'Show me a [. . .] function', with the name of an organ inserted. At this given signal, the children will be expected to stand on the spot wherever they are in the room and to mime a function of the named organ. For example, following 'Show me a lungs function', the children will stand still and breathe in and out, or pretend to smoke, or pretend to sing.

45 Female or male?

Ⓟ **Purpose**

To enable children to identify body parts, their correct names and to which gender they apply.

> **Suggested age range**

Older Juniors.

⫽ **Materials needed**

Class set of the worksheet on p.123. For each group, a copy of both the male and the female anatomy (see pp. 128–129), large sheet of blank paper.

◔ **Approximate timing**

30 minutes minimum.

▶ **What else it relates to**

Body talk
Naming the frame
Fishing for facts
Getting organised
Checking out the facts

▲▲ **Numbers involved**

Whole class, working in small groups if appropriate.

What to do

The teacher divides the class into groups of four or five (using an idea from Chapter 3). Each child in the group has a worksheet listing various parts of the body.

The task for the group is to decide which words on the list apply to women and which to men. Some will apply to both. The words could be marked 'F', 'M', or 'B' or perhaps coded in different colours. The group should reach a decision for each word with which everyone is happy.

The teacher then gives a large blank sheet of paper to each group, on which they should draw two outlines, one of a man and one of a woman. They must label the outlines with all of the terms from the worksheet. After they have done this, the anatomical drawings are given out, in order to check that the group's version is correct.

45 Female or male?

Decide which of these parts belong to males (M), females (F) or both (B):

Ovaries

Testicles

Penis

Pituitary gland

Vagina

Urethra

Fallopian tubes

Breasts

Nipples

Scrotum

Pubic hair

Cervix

---

45 Outline of male

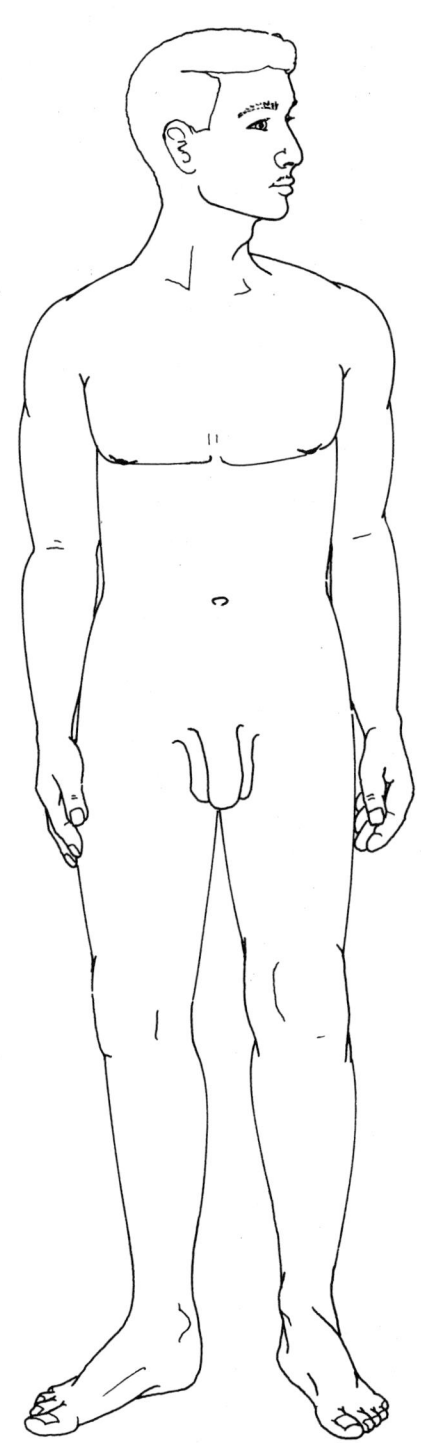

45 Outline of female

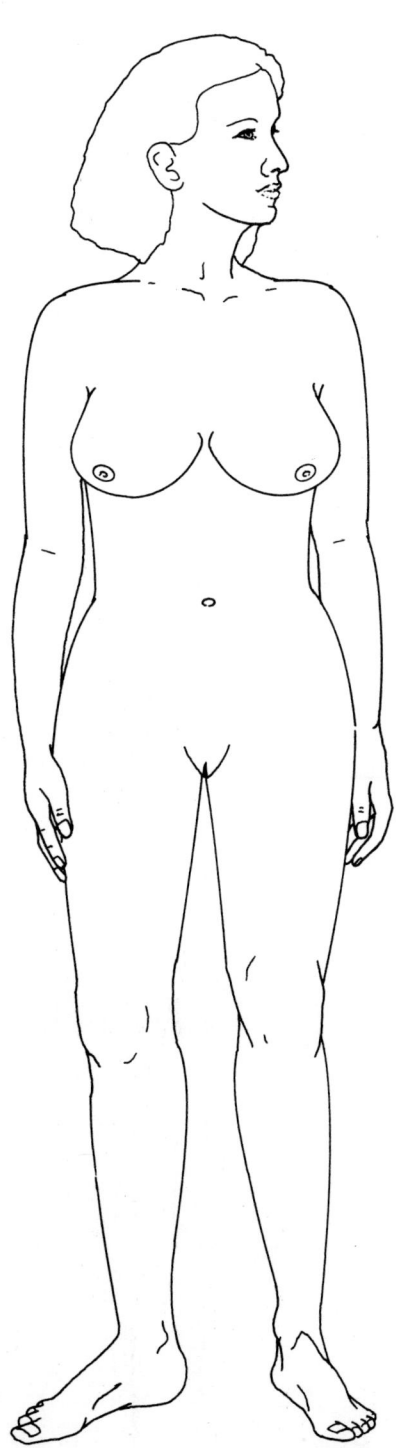

45 Internal organs of the body (male)

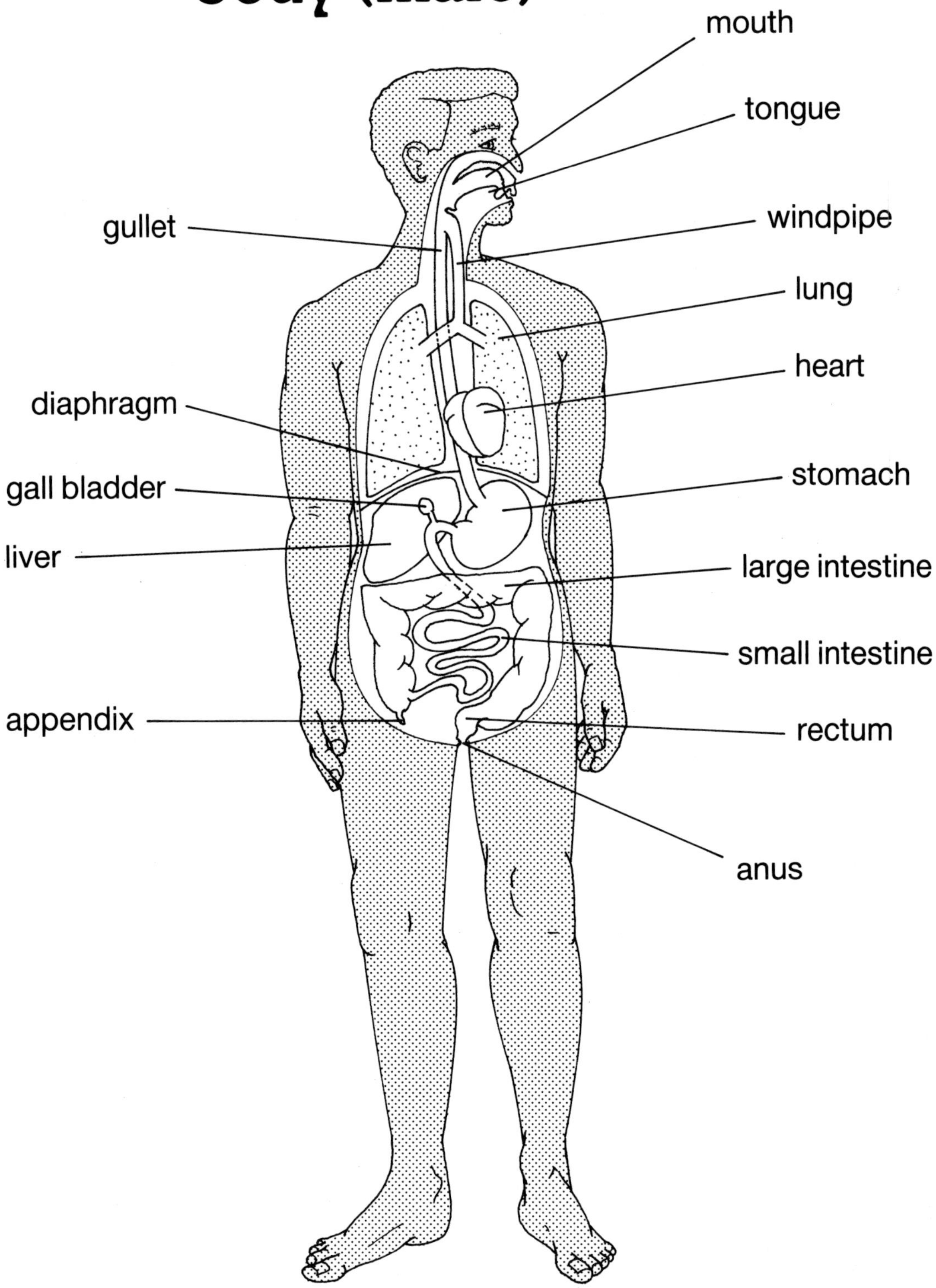

mouth

tongue

gullet

windpipe

lung

heart

diaphragm

stomach

gall bladder

liver

large intestine

small intestine

appendix

rectum

anus

45 Internal organs of the body (female)

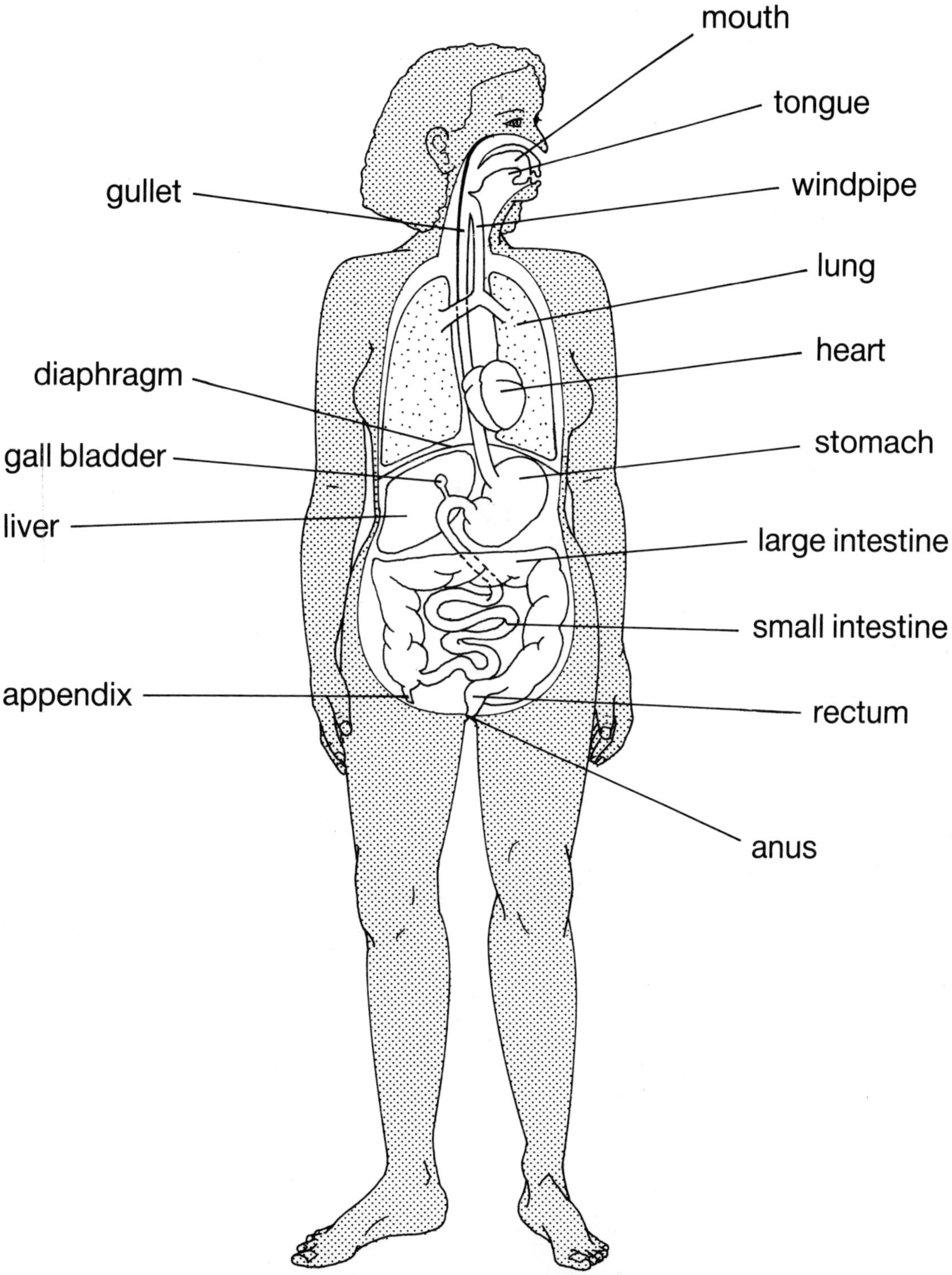

mouth

tongue

gullet

windpipe

lung

heart

diaphragm

stomach

gall bladder

liver

large intestine

small intestine

appendix

rectum

anus

45 Male anatomy

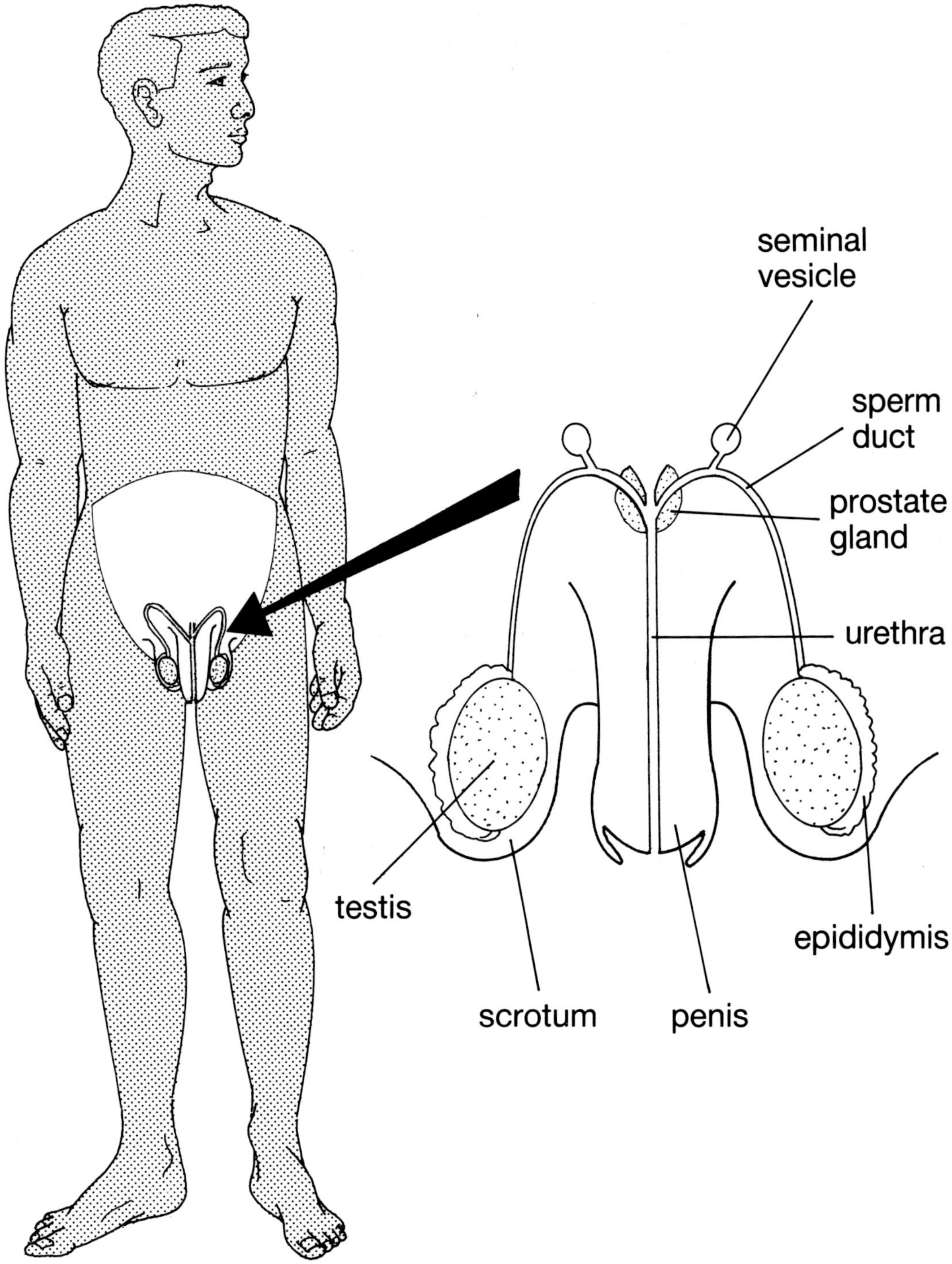

seminal
vesicle

sperm
duct

prostate
gland

urethra

testis

epididymis

scrotum   penis

45 Female anatomy

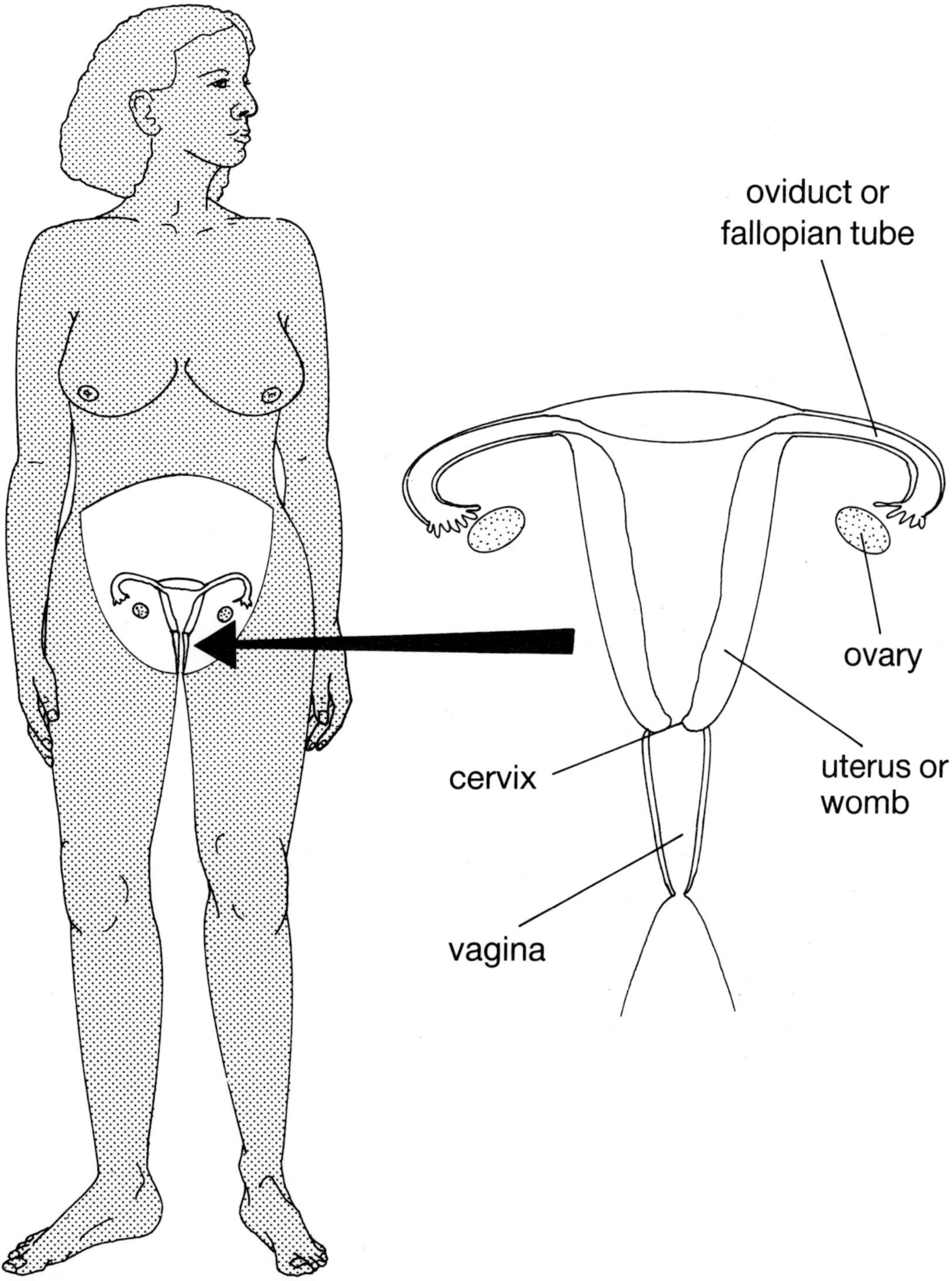

oviduct or
fallopian tube

ovary

cervix

uterus or
womb

vagina

46 Guess the baby

℗ Purpose

To demonstrate to children that, as we grow, we change in what we can do and in our responsibilities.

＞ Suggested age range

Any age.

✏ Materials needed

Photograph from home, display space, sheet of paper, pens.

◑ Approximate timing

30 minutes.

▶ What else it relates to

A day in the life
Retrographs
Good time lines
Puberty quiz
Puberty!

👥 Numbers involved

Whole class.

What to do

The teacher asks the class to bring in photographs of themselves when they were younger. The teacher may wish to bring in photographs of her/himself and may ask colleagues to do the same.

These photographs are mixed and the children are asked to identify which photograph belongs to which child or teacher.

The teacher then asks each child to produce a piece of work to go under his/her picture. The following headings may be useful:

When I was this age I could do . . .
and I was responsible for . . .

Now I can . . .
I am responsible for . . .

In five years' time I will be able to . . .
and I will be responsible for . . .

47 A day in the life

Ⓟ **Purpose**

To identify responsibilities and roles.

To enable children to become aware of their own responsibilities and those of others.

To increase awareness of how responsibilities change with age.

> **Suggested age range**

All ages.

✏ **Materials needed**

Paper, pencils, art materials, Blu-tak.

▶ **What else it relates to**

Guess the baby
Retrographs

◕ **Approximate timing**

30 minutes.

👤👤 **Numbers involved**

Whole class.

What to do

The class begins by having a brainstorm about all of the activities that people have to do during a day, e.g. getting up, washing.

Having produced the list, the children can work in small groups to sort out the brainstorm into a chronological order. The teacher may suggest that they do illustrations.

Once all of the class has produced illustrations, these can be displayed in chronological order around the room, using Blu-tak. The teacher might then form groups of three and feed in the question: 'At what age should someone be responsible for these activities?'

Using a short amount of time for discussion, the groups of three write down on paper the ages for each activity illustrated.

At a given signal from the teacher, the groups are asked to hold up their age cards for each activity. Any differences of opinion between the groups can be used as a stimulus for further discussion.

Of course, this can be repeated for different illustrations.

A further development might be for groups to discuss their feelings about having responsibilities at certain ages.

48 Retrographs

Ⓟ Purpose

To highlight changes in what we can do and in our responsibilities.
To see ourselves in relationship to others.

> Suggested age range

Any Junior group.

⫽ Materials needed

Large sheets of paper, small pieces of paper, felt-tipped pens, pencils.

◗ Approximate timing

30 minutes.

▶ What else it relates to

Guess the baby
A day in the life
Tracking time
Good time lines
Puberty quiz
Puberty!

▲▲ Numbers involved

Whole class, individually then in groups.

——— What to do ———

The teacher asks the children to draw a long line on the sheet of paper. This will be a time line. They should put the year in which they were born at the beginning of the line and the present year about two-thirds of the way along, as shown here:

/_____/_____
Year born   Present year

The teacher then asks the children to brainstorm the activities that they have learned to do so far and also what they expect to do in the future (e.g. walk, read, talk, have babies, have a period, drive, get a job, have a special friend).

The children are asked to write out the words from the brainstorm, using one small piece of paper for each activity.

They should place these along the time line in the appropriate positions denoting the time that they learned/expect to do these things.

The children can then work in pairs or threes to compare their ideas.

The teacher will be able to encourage class discussion by such questions as:

'Do you agree with each other?'
'What parts do you not agree about?'
'What have you learned?'

49 Tracking time

Ⓟ Purpose

To focus on personal, local and global changes and to record these in a variety of forms.

To develop a sense of time.

To recognise the differences and similarities between people.

＞ Suggested age range

Any age.

Materials needed

Time line round room or along wall, divided into years and going back as far as the birth year of the oldest child.

Individual time lines, large sheets of paper and pens for 'trigger session'.

◕ Approximate timing

Introductory lesson: 30 minutes, then the time line can be revisited as often as required.

▶ What else it relates to

Guess the baby

Retrographs

Family favourites

Good time lines

Numbers involved

Whole class.

―――――― What to do ――――――

The teacher and children make a time line for classroom display, leaving large spaces between each year. Below the time line the teacher may put up a certain coloured piece of paper and say that this sheet is for personal memories of the class. Underneath the 'personal memory' paper, the class may wish to have 'local memories'. Below that there may be a third colour of paper for 'global events'.

Having done this, the teacher asks the children to work in groups of three or four (using ideas from Chapter 3). They must list important events that happen in people's lives (e.g. moving schools, births, marriages, illnesses). After 4–5 minutes, these ideas are shared as a whole class.

Once the ideas have been collected together, the teacher might ask the children to record major events on their individual time lines.

When the children are ready, they work in pairs to negotiate which important events should be illustrated on the class time line. They can help each other to produce their work.

The children can be encouraged to bring in personal artefacts (e.g. identification tags from birth) to add to the display at the appropriate date. Children's written personal memories can be displayed, along with the teacher's. Parents and the local community can be invited to contribute. The teacher may wish to use the 'Visitor experience' for this (see pages 60–61).

The global events line can be filled out by developing research skills with children, who may also devise questionnaires to elicit other information from adults.

50 Family favourites

Ⓟ **Purpose**

To identify what groups do together.
To celebrate family events.

> **Suggested age range**

Any age.

✐ **Materials needed**

Paper, art materials, pencils.

◑ **Approximate timing**

30 minutes.

▶ **What else it relates to**

Tracking time
Good time lines

👥 **Numbers involved**

Whole class.

What to do

The teacher asks the class to list individually the things that they like to do together as a family. Younger children may do this in picture form. This activity can be carried out without reference to other children and without letting classmates see.

In pairs (or in a larger group setting), the children mime the activities so that other people can guess what they are doing.

The children can then write about happy family times, or draw pictures, or make a 'Thank You' card for a member of their family.

51 Good time lines

(P) Purpose

To offer the opportunity to share memories with each other.
To develop a sense of time.
To encourage positive affirmation.

> Suggested age range

Junior age range.

Materials needed

Large pieces of paper,
felt-tipped pens.

● Approximate timing

30 minutes.

▶ What else it relates to

Guess the baby
Retrographs
Tracking time
Family favourites

Numbers involved

Whole class, initially
working alone, then in
pairs/threes.

What to do

The children are asked to form 'friendship' pairs or threes. (This should be done sensitively. If there is any child who might be isolated at this point, the teacher may wish to ask the children to form threes according to a different criterion.) Once the groups have been formed, the children are asked to work alone initially but to think about the other member(s) of their group. The teacher will need to feed in suggestions to guide the activity. These would include:

'Think back to the time when you first met.'
'Think about the times that you remember sharing with the person/people in your group.'

The children are then asked to produce a time line of moments that they remember. They should draw a long line on their piece of paper, putting the year in which they were born at one end and 'Now' at the other end. They should mark off the years in between. They write their memories at the relevant point on the time line.

They can then share their time lines.

Variation

This same activity can be carried out to enable the children to reflect on memories of the times that they have shared in their family group.

52 Forces of persuasion

Purpose

To identify what influences our decisions.

To increase awareness of personal responsibility.

Suggested age range

Older Juniors.

Materials needed

Paper, pens.

Approximate timing

30 minutes+

What else it relates to

Plotting people
Risk factor
How I keep myself safe
Body talk

Numbers involved

Whole class.

What to do

The teacher introduces the children to the idea of 'force-field analysis'. This involves them in identifying forces which encourage them to behave in a particular way.

For example, should they go to the woods after dark if a close friend insists that they do?

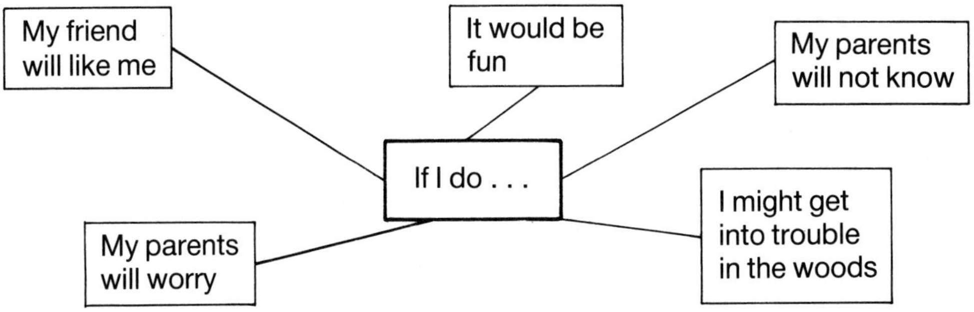

This can lead to a session where children will be asked to write about situations which present dilemmas for them, such as:

The time that I was tempted to steal . . .
The time that I found some money . . .
My friends said they would not play with me unless I . . .
I should have been looking after my little sister but instead I wanted to . . .

53 Puberty quiz

Ⓟ **Purpose**

To assess children's knowledge of puberty.

> **Suggested age range**

Upper Juniors.

✏ **Materials needed**

Photocopies of worksheet on p.140, pens. Books for research.

◗ **Approximate timing**

30 minutes.

▶ **What else it relates to**

Guess the baby
Retrograph
Puberty!

👥 **Numbers involved**

Whole class, individually then in pairs.

What to do

The teacher distributes the quiz and asks the children to respond to the true/false statements. Once this is done, the teacher may choose to go through the questions with the children or to allow them to compare answers.

If the children are going to be encouraged to research the answers for themselves, then the teacher must ensure that there is a variety of material for children to use (see Resources section in Chapter 7).

We must stress that it is very important that any inaccurate understanding is addressed. We are very aware that children become anxious if they feel that they are different in any way. We have always tried to celebrate differences as part of our teaching.

53 Puberty quiz

Read the sentences below. Decide whether each one is true or false.

If you think it is true, circle the 'T'; if you think it is false, circle the 'F'.

1 All girls' bodies begin to change at age 11. T F

2 Puberty comes from a word meaning 'to become hairy'. T F

3 Girls start puberty before boys. T F

4 Girls have periods once a month at the beginning of puberty. T F

5 Menstruation happens so that girls can choose to have babies in the future. T F

6 Changes happen because of a gland in our head. T F

7 As our bodies change, so do our feelings. T F

8 There is no need to worry about the size of our sexual organs. T F

9 Sperm comes out of the body through the boy's penis. T F

10 Sometimes sperm comes out of the body at night. T F

11 Playing with the sexual organs is bad for you. T F

12 All boys will end up with deep voices. T F

13 All boys will grow hairy chests. T F

14 The hormone that causes the changes is different in girls and boys. T F

15 You have to wash even more carefully at puberty. T F

54 Puberty!

Ⓟ Purpose

To increase children's understanding of developmental changes during puberty.

＞ Suggested age range

Upper Juniors.

✍ Materials needed

Photocopies of all pictures and statements (see pp.142–144) cut up for each group.

◕ Approximate timing

30 minutes.

▶ What else it relates to

Guess the baby
Retrographs
Puberty quiz

👥 Numbers involved

Groups of six.

What to do

The teacher distributes the picture cards so that each child has one picture. The statement cards are placed face down in a pile in the middle. The purpose of the game is explained. This is to collect statement cards which relate to each picture.

Each child takes it in turn to take a card from the pile. S/he can keep the card if it relates to her/his picture. If not, other children in the group can claim the card by being the first to call out 'Puberty!'.

This process continues until all of the cards have been placed under the appropriate picture. There are no 'right answers', since some of the cards will apply to more than one picture, so the game will involve negotiation and co-operation between children.

Variation/follow-up activity

In groups, the children make a cube out of card (see diagram on p.143).

On each face of the cube, they stick one of the cut-out line drawings from p.142.

They take turns in rolling the cube and then trying to match the image which ends up on top to whichever statement cards they think are appropriate. The cards could be strewn about in a random fashion for this.

This method requires a lot more discussion and agreement from the children.

54 Puberty!:

Changes in girls

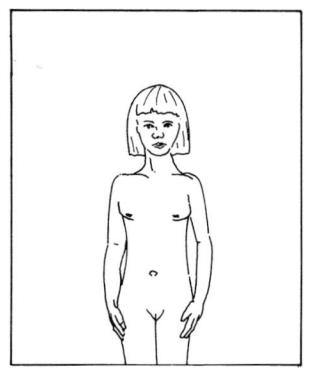 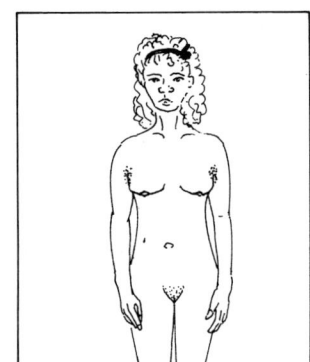 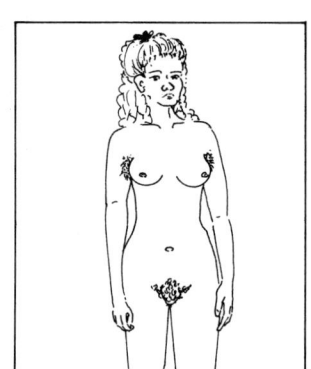

Changes in boys

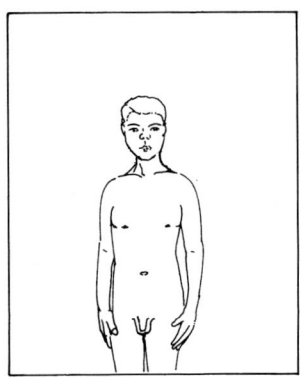 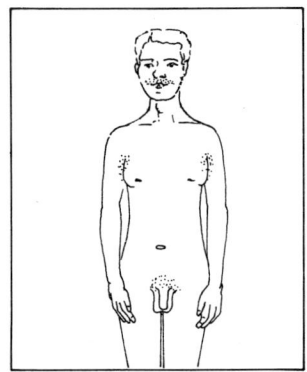 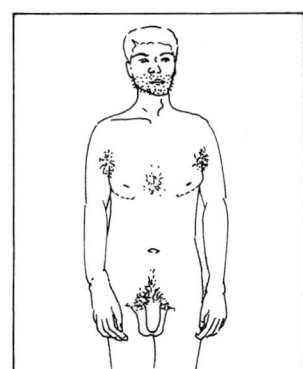

54 Puberty!: cube shape

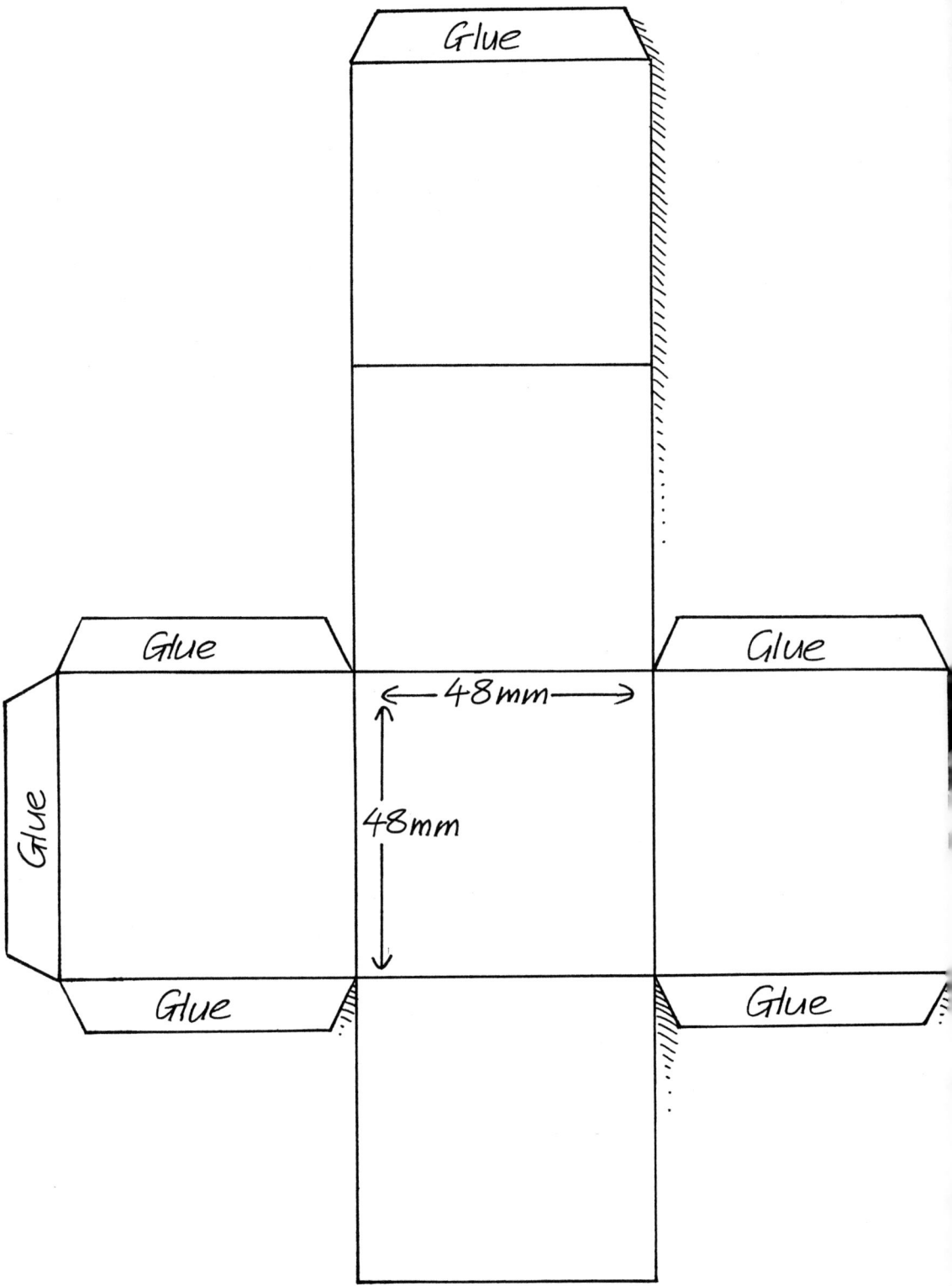

54 'Puberty!': statements

I have developed breasts.

My breasts have not begun to develop.

My breasts have begun to develop.

My hips are starting to get rounder.

I have noticed that I sweat more.

I need to wash my body more often.

My voice is changing.

My voice is now quite deep.

My shoulders and chest are now quite broad.

My periods have not started yet.

I am having periods regularly.

My periods have started but are not regular yet.

Hair is starting to grow under my arms.

Hair is starting to grow around my penis.

Hair is starting to grow around the opening to my vagina.

There is hair under my arms and around my penis.

There is hair under my arms and around the opening to my vagina.

I have no hair on my face.

Hair is starting to grow on my face.

I need to shave regularly.

I feel sexually attracted to another person.

My penis is still quite small.

My penis and testicles are starting to grow.

☐ Dealing with menstruation in the classroom

A considerable number of girls will have started their periods by the time that they leave primary school, and so teachers should be aware that girls may begin menstruating in school time and should be prepared for dealing with it. If it is the first time, a girl may be totally unprepared for what is happening. She may be upset by the experience, particularly if the rest of her class do not know much either and she is rushed away to the medical room and the whole episode is not referred to again.

What can help?

Teachers who teach 9–11 year olds could meet in a group to discuss their feelings about the topic and suggest helpful strategies. Male teachers should not be excluded, as their attitudes to the emerging sexuality of their pupils can be of crucial importance. An unhelpful or disparaging remark can do untold damage.

Obviously it would be preferable if children could be taught about the onset of puberty well in advance of its happening, but we must be realistic. It is likely to be taught in the last year of primary school. Both boys and girls need to know about it. It is not just a girl's subject.

Recommended is a video called *Having A Period*. It features a young woman talking to her younger sister and brother about menstruation in a very matter-of-fact way (see Resources section in Chapter 7).

The school nurse can be an excellent ally and resource in teaching about menstruation, so do remember to include her in planning sessions and in any staff consideration of sex education in general.

It is very important to be positive about menstruation rather than being negative. This applies to all aspects of teaching about puberty and sexuality.

In other societies we find a much healthier attitude towards menstruation. A girl's first period is greeted positively and is celebrated, whereas in western culture it is seen as something of a nuisance and definitely not to be alluded to in general conversation.

Whilst not suggesting that we introduce menstruation parties into the classroom, we do think that much can be done in the primary school to promote positive attitudes to menstruation. Just having it discussed without embarrassment can be a start.

55 What is menstruation?

As we grow up, our bodies change in different ways. Some of these changes happen on the outside and some on the inside. See if you can make a list of the things that happen to girls:

Things that happen outside the body

Things that happen inside the body

When a girl reaches puberty, she will start to *menstruate* or *have periods*. It is perfectly normal for this to happen any time between the ages of 8 and 16.

The *ovaries* begin to release egg cells, normally one every 28 days or so. The egg passes along the *fallopian tube* into the *womb*. Every month, the womb gets a special lining, in case the egg is fertilised by a sperm and starts to grow into a baby.

Most of the time, this does not happen and the special lining is not required, so it passes out of the vagina. This is called *having a period* and normally takes between 3 and 6 days. It happens to all girls and women until they reach the age of about 50–55, although this varies from woman to woman.

The amount of blood is actually quite small although sometimes it seems a lot.

Dealing with a period soon becomes part of a girl's everyday life. She will need to wear a pad (sometimes called a sanitary towel) or vaginal tampon (a small, tightly compressed roll of cotton fibre) to soak up the blood and protect the clothing.

There is a wide range of pads and tampons available from chemists and supermarkets. Ask your mother, older sister or an older female friend about the various kinds available, and see if you can try out a few of them. Tampons may take some practice until you become used to them.

At first, periods are usually irregular but they generally settle down after a few months. Girls get used to knowing when their periods are going to come, so that they can be prepared. Sometimes girls and women find that they feel irritable or suffer from stomach cramps before a period. This is called Pre-Menstrual Syndrome (or PMS) and is perfectly normal. There is help and advice available.

Where do you think that help and advice might be available?

56 Why wash?

℗ **Purpose**

To encourage an understanding of the need for personal hygiene.
To prioritise the usefulness of different items.
To increase awareness of the cost of hygiene and the relative value of cost.

❯ **Suggested age range**

Juniors.

✎ **Materials needed**

Photocopies of worksheet on p.149, art materials, paper, pens/pencils.

◕ **Approximate timing**

45 minutes+

▶ **What else it relates to**

What is menstruation?
Kim's game

👥 **Numbers involved**

Alone/pairs/whole class.

What to do

The teacher distributes the worksheet and encourages the children to work alone on the parts that can be done in the classroom. (The teacher must point out that some of the work will need to be carried out at home.)

The children can be encouraged to work in pairs to share their ideas.

When the children are working as a whole group, the teacher will be able to amplify their ideas and add to them.

56 Why wash?

We wash to get rid of . . .

If we do not wash . . .

When we need to wash . . .

What parts of the body need careful washing?

- List items that we use to keep us clean. Sort them into groups:

  VERY IMPORTANT   USEFUL   NOT VERY IMPORTANT

- Draw pictures of all of the things that keep us clean.
- Make a hygiene poster.
- Find out how much it costs to keep you clean. List items that you might find in your home. Find out the prices. How long do they last? Are they all essential?

57 Kim's game

Ⓟ **Purpose**

To increase awareness of the importance of hygiene, and to identify hygienic items that may need to be used.

> **Suggested age range**

Upper Juniors.

✏ **Materials needed**

Tray with objects on it (including bra, sanitary towel, tampon, soap, towel, deodorant, shaving equipment, jockstrap, shampoo), a cover for the tray, large sheets of paper, pens, pencils, art materials.

▶ **What else it relates to**

What is menstruation?
Why wash?

◕ **Approximate timing**

30 minutes+

👥 **Numbers involved**

Small groups of five or six.

What to do

The teacher explains that this is a memory game. The children are going to be given 30 *seconds* to look at objects on a tray, then the tray is removed and they must try to list them on the large sheet of paper.

The large sheet of paper is divided into three sections:

For Female Use   For Male Use   For Both Female and Male Use

The children study the tray for 30 seconds. Once it has been removed the children work together to list the objects in the different categories.

When this has been done, the children are encouraged to discuss what the purpose of each object is.

Then they can work alone or in pairs, designing a poster about hygiene.

·6·

What's love got to do with it?

There are many reasons why people have sex. See if you can add to our brainstorm:

Pleasure

Power

Pain

To have children

To feel good about oneself

To impress others

Peer pressure

Societal pressure

Curiosity

Cultural norms

Media pressure

To act out our fantasies

To express love

☐ Introduction

The whole area of sexual activity and attraction is one of the most difficult for adults. As course leaders, we have worked with many teachers and we do recognise that it raises many issues, including one's stance on morality, acceptable forms of behaviour, embarrassment, and difficulties with forms of language. It is no wonder that it is not an easy area to present to young children. This is particularly true when we recognise that primary school children are at different levels of experience and development. We do understand that many adults may find it offensive not only if we suggest that sexual activity can be enjoyable, even within a marriage bond, but also if we acknowledge that people of the same sex form relationships. However, it is part of the real world, and our role as teachers is to help the children to make sense of what is going on. If we want the children in our care to form relationships which are right for them, it can be argued that they will need to know why people are attracted to each other and that there are many ways to express feelings.

In doing this, we must be aware of the law. In the 1986 Education Act, we are told that children need to be taught about sex 'in such a manner as to encourage those pupils to have due regard to moral considerations and the value of family life'. Unfortunately, those who worded the Act omitted to go on to explain what they meant by a 'family'. It might be comforting to have in mind the idea of the nuclear family – mum, dad and a couple of children – when we are talking about families in the classroom, but it would not be realistic and might well be downright offensive to some.

There may be a few geographical areas left where the majority of families are of the type already mentioned, but they are decidedly not in the majority when we look at the country as a whole. Statistics show that 1 family in 7 is now headed by a single parent.

If you are doubtful about any of this, just think about your own class. How many of them live in the traditional nuclear family set-up? It is likely that several live in quite different situations. Perhaps one lives with a single mother or father; or with a mother or father and a grandparent. Some will live with a parent who has divorced and remarried, so will be coping with a step-parent and possibly step-sisters and brothers. Others will be living with parents who are not married, or with a parent who may have a succession of temporary relationships. Sometimes the family may consist of a parent who is in a long-term relationship with someone of the same sex. And do not forget the children who are living with a foster family, or who may have been adopted. Parenting can be carried out just as successfully by people who are not necessarily the child's natural parents. It is no wonder that defining 'family' is not merely difficult but well nigh impossible! Thus, it is not surprising that teachers tend to choose 'safer' sex lessons!

In this chapter we are offering a variety of approaches to what is potentially a minefield. Even if you choose to use a video or printed resource to disseminate information, it is worthwhile to consider ways in which children may be given the opportunity to construct ideas before presenting your didactic input. Suggestions about how to do this are presented. It is too easy to make assumptions about what the children know or do not know, and it is important to consider the mismatch between the delivered and received curriculum. We do advocate that teachers should encourage children to create their own agenda. In this way, what they want to know about is made explicit. The questions that they are *not* asking are an indication of areas that might need to be covered.

Some teachers will be thinking that homosexuality is something that need not be mentioned in a primary school, perhaps on the grounds that it is outside the children's experience. This is a view that needs to be challenged, not only for the reason given earlier about family life, but also for other reasons.

Even if you yourself are not a reader of the tabloid press, you will be aware that such papers are in the homes of some of your pupils and that they abound with vitriolic statements about same-sex relationships (sometimes referred to as 'homophobia'). Children, like adults, are not immune to this kind of insidious approach.

Similarly, when you are on playground duty, you will be aware of what sometimes crops up in children's conversations: words such as 'poofters', 'queers' and 'lezzies' are often used as terms of abuse but come in most cases from a background of ignorance, fear and prejudice.

We feel strongly that teachers are in an excellent position to challenge prejudice and discrimination when it rears its head in the classroom. This is especially so where children are being taught in ways which encourage them to explore their feelings, to acknowledge their differences, and to be supportive of one another. We already do this with regard to issues such as racism, sexism and disability. Hatred and intolerance flourish unless they are questioned and rigorously opposed.

Above all, we must return to one of the most important aspects of our work as teachers: we do want children to like themselves and to feel confident.

58 Suggestion box

℗ Purpose

To enable children to ask questions in a non-threatening way.

> Suggested age range

Any age.

✐ Materials needed

Postbox, blank pieces of paper, pencils.

◑ Approximate timing

No fixed time.

▶ What else it relates to

Questions in a hat

👥 Numbers involved

Individual.

What to do

The teacher explains that a suggestion box is going to be placed in the classroom for a number of weeks. It will be available for the children to 'post' any questions and ideas for their sex education lessons.

This is to enable the children to express their thoughts and questions anonymously.

These points can be dealt with at any appropriate time during the school week.

59 Questions in a hat

Ⓟ Purpose

To allow the children to ask 'difficult' questions in a non-threatening way.

To enable the children to set the agenda for sex education.

> Suggested age range

Upper Juniors (who are all able to read).

⫽ Materials needed

Blank pieces of paper, pencils, a hat.

◕ Approximate timing

20 minutes. (A much longer time should be allocated if the teacher is to deal with the questions in the same session.)

▶ What else it relates to

Suggestion box

Numbers involved

Whole class.

_____ What to do _____

The whole class sits in a circle. The teacher distributes paper and a pen to each child and asks the children to write down questions about sex which they want to have answered.

When the children have done this, they fold up their questions, which are collected in a hat.

The questions are then redistributed and each child reads out the question that s/he has received.

The teacher may choose to answer the questions right away and might use the children themselves to assist in this task. Alternatively, after the children have read out the questions, the teacher may collect them in and use them to prepare for a future session.

Variation

This process can be used to allow the children to express their ideas without embarrassment, and is adaptable to many other situations.

60 Videowatch

We are going to watch something about..........................

In pairs, discuss what questions are in your head at the moment about this subject. Together make a list of things that you already know about, things that you are not sure about, and things that you would like to know more about.

Already know	Not sure about	Would like to know more about

Now that you have seen the programme, put a tick beside those things on your list that have been covered.

Has everything which you were not sure about, or felt that you wanted to know more about, been covered?

Did the programme raise anything which was not on your list?

61 Attraction reaction

Ⓟ **Purpose**

To explore what children feel about expressing attraction.
To offer the teacher information about the children's values.

\> **Suggested age range**

Upper Juniors.

✏ **Materials needed**

Photocopies of list of words (see p.159), coloured pencils or pens.

◕ **Approximate timing**

30 minutes.

▶ **What else it relates to**

The feelings collection
Reading our feelings

👥 **Numbers involved**

Whole class.

_____ **What to do** _____

A copy of the list of words should be given to each child.

The teacher asks the children to think about these words in terms of how people show that they are attracted to one another. The children are then asked to say which words they consider to indicate a strong attraction, a mild attraction, or no attraction. This they can do by circling the words in different colours, to indicate the different levels, and by providing a key to the colours.

When the children have done this, the teacher asks them to form pairs and to compare and discuss their sheets. Do they have the same ideas? What are the differences?

The sheets can be handed in at the end of the lesson. This can inform the teacher of the children's values. With this knowledge, the teacher will be able to construct future discussions.

61 Attraction reaction

Kissing   Stroking   Tickling   Comforting

Biting   Cuddling   Winking   Licking

Singing   Gazing   Eating   Blowing kisses

Talking   Waving   Smiling   Hugging

62 Reading our feelings

Ⓟ **Purpose**

To identify a range of ways in which people show their feelings.
To show that this is sometimes different for children and adults.
To consider how people sometimes do one thing when they mean another.

❯ **Suggested age range**

8+

✏ **Materials needed**

Photocopies of sheets A and B (see pp. 162–163), pens or pencils.

◕ **Approximate timing**

30 minutes.

▶ **What else it relates to**

The feelings collection
Attraction reaction

👥 **Numbers involved**

Whole class, divided into small groups if appropriate.

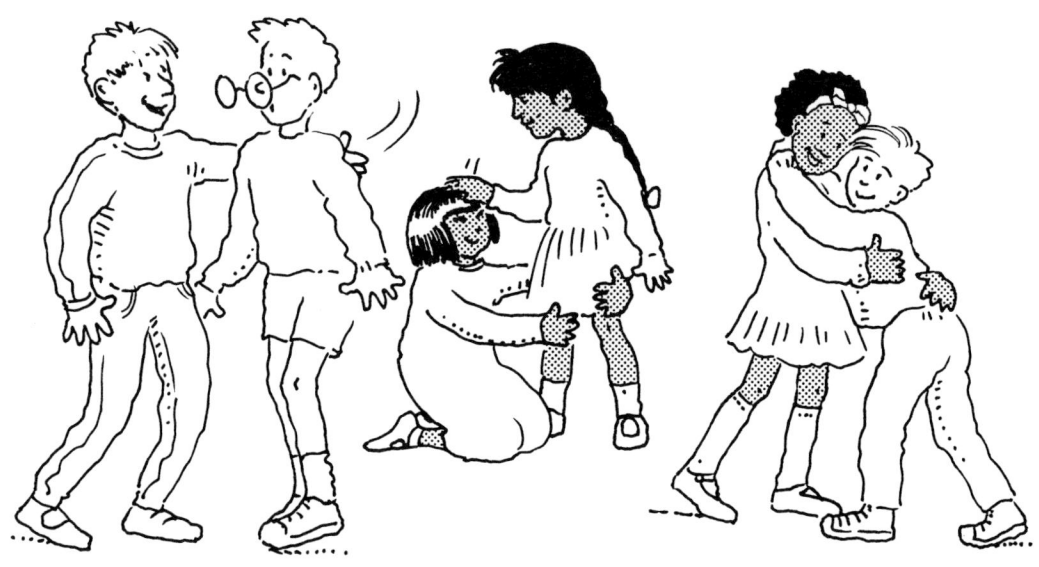

What to do

The teacher introduces the activity by talking about ways in which we show our feelings towards each other. For instance, if someone came and hit us hard, we might reasonably assume that that person did not like us.

The teacher distributes sheets A and B. One half of the class (A) considers how other people behave towards them, when those people like them and when they do not like them. The other half of the class (B) chooses an adult whom they know and thinks of ways in which people show their good and bad feelings for that adult.

The children can do this activity on their own, in pairs, or in small groups.

If they do it individually, they can join up with two or three others and share their findings. Then each small group who has done activity A joins with another group who has done activity B, and they share their findings.

Trigger questions, which the teacher might want to ask in the whole group feedback, include:

'When people show you that they like you, do they show it to adults in a different way?'
'Why do you think this is?'
'Do we all show our feelings in the same way?'
'Can you think of ways in which people behave towards you which are meant well but which you don't like?'

The teacher could give an example: 'When I was a child, my aunt always patted me on the head. I hated it.'
'Are there any situations that you can think of where someone behaves in a certain way towards you but they mean the opposite of what they are doing?'

62 Reading our feelings (A)

People show me they like me by . . .

People show me they do not like me by . . .

62 Reading our feelings (B)

Think of an adult you know. How do other people show that they like this person?

How do people show that they do not like this person?

63 Checking out the facts

℗ Purpose

To offer a model of the type of worksheet that teachers can produce for their children.

To enable children to test out their knowledge of sexual activity and reproduction.

> Suggested age range

Upper Juniors.

∥ Materials needed

Photocopies of worksheet (see p.165) cut in two, paper, pens.

◔ Approximate timing

30 minutes.

▶ What else it relates to

Body talk
Naming the frame
Fishing for facts
Getting organised
Female or male?
Know-how

▲▲ Numbers involved

Small groups of two or three.

_____ What to do _____

The teacher asks the children to look at the words and to categorise them into groups which relate to each other.

The teacher may then wish to ask the children to record these on a piece of paper, so that any misunderstandings can be rectified.

The children can be asked to form ends of sentences, using the beginnings listed at the foot of the worksheet.

63 Checking out the facts

Womb	Penis	Testicles	Female
Where sperm is stored	Where babies grow	Male	Nine months
Ovum	Egg	Where sperm comes out of the body	Navel
Umbilical cord	Vagina	Scrotum	Period
About every 28 days	Where eggs are stored	Ovaries	Pregnancy

Copy these sentence openings, one at a time, and add as much as you can, using words from this activity:

I know that females have . . .

I know that males have . . .

As a general rule, a woman will have a period . . .

Babies grow . . .

Now make up some sentences of your own. Try to use some of the words from this activity.

64 Circle round the truth

Ⓟ **Purpose**

To offer a model of the type of worksheet that teachers can produce for their children.

To assess children's understanding of sexual penetration.

> **Suggested age range**

Upper Juniors.

Materials needed

Photocopies of worksheet on p.167.

◐ **Approximate timing**

20 minutes.

▶ **What else it relates to**

Any work on sexual activity.

Numbers involved

Alone then in pairs.

What to do

After giving children some information about sexual activity, the teacher makes the worksheet available to the children.

The teacher may wish to encourage the children to write down any issues that have been raised by the activity. These can be put into the class suggestion box or used in a 'questions in a hat' activity (see pp. 155 and 156 for details of these).

64 Circle round the truth

Sexual penetration is one form of sexual activity.

Put a circle around the statements below which you think are true. Compare your answers with a partner.

1   For sexual penetration to take place, a man's penis has to be hard.

2   For sexual penetration to take place, a man has to lie on top of the other person.

3   For sexual penetration to take place, a condom has to be worn.

4   People have sex only when they are in love with each other.

5   People have sexual intercourse to have babies.

6   At some point during sexual activity, body fluids are produced.

7   The penis cannot produce semen and urine at the same time.

8   A climax for a man is when sperm comes out of the body.

9   People are noisy when they have sexual intercourse.

65 What is masturbation?

Ⓟ **Purpose**

To offer a model of a worksheet that teachers may use/adapt/create to meet the needs of their children.

To offer information about masturbation (in this case).

To offer trigger statements to encourage children to explore their knowledge.

> **Suggested age range**

Upper Juniors.

✎ **Materials needed**

Photocopies of worksheet (p.169) and answer sheet (p.170).

◑ **Approximate timing**

30 minutes.

▶ **What else it relates to**

This is a model worksheet. It may be used for any subject where information must be given and knowledge assessed.

In this case, the masturbation worksheet relates to any input on sexual activity.

Both the 'Suggestion box' and the 'Questions in a hat' activities offer non-threatening structures for the children to express fears/worries/concerns/questions.

👥 **Numbers involved**

Individuals or small groups.

What to do

The worksheet is distributed for children to work on alone or in small groups.

This kind of worksheet can be offered as an introduction to a particular topic. The responses of the children will inform the teacher of learning experiences that need to be addressed.

Alternatively, it can be used to assess the children's perceptions after other inputs on the subject have been given.

65 What is masturbation?

As our bodies change, we may start to have sexual feelings towards other people and about ourselves. Certain parts of our bodies can become exciting to touch. One of these parts is called the *genital area*. For boys this is the penis and testicles, and for girls it is the area around the opening to the vagina, in particular the clitoris.

Some people enjoy rubbing these areas in a certain way. If they do this for a while, they may reach a moment when it is very exciting indeed. Fluids may be produced by the body at this stage. For a male, this will be semen which comes out of the end of the penis. For a female, this will be vaginal fluid. It is called this because it is produced in the vagina.

Read the questions below then read the answers on the other sheet.

Find the answer which fits each question and write the letter in the space below.

1   To my knowledge I have never masturbated. Is this okay?

2   Can it hurt me?

3   Does everybody do it?

4   Why have I not seen anybody doing it?

5   Do adults do it?

1   5   ....

2   6   ....

3   7   ....

4   ....

Use the suggestion box in the classroom if you have any more questions.

65 What is masturbation?

Answers

A No. People used to think masturbating could harm you. This is not true.

B It is impossible to say, because people do not often talk about it.

C Yes. It is perfectly normal whether people choose to masturbate or not.

D Most people choose to masturbate in private. This is important because it shows that they respect other people's privacy too. It is against the law to do it in public.

E Yes, masturbation is something that can be done at any time, by any age group.

66 Happy birthways!

(P) Purpose

To enable the children to understand that babies of different animals grow either inside or outside the body.

> Suggested age range

Top Infants upwards.

Materials needed

Photocopies of worksheet on p.172, pencils, art materials, books for children's own research.

Approximate timing

30 minutes.

▶ What else it relates to

Link the baby with its carer
Know-how
Stages of pregnancy

Numbers involved

Individual activity.

What to do

The teacher may choose to use this worksheet to reinforce the children's knowledge about birth.

Books should be available for the children to carry out the activities at the bottom of the pupil worksheet.

66 Happy birthways!

The babies of different animals are born in different ways. Some hatch from an egg. The mother lays this. The baby can grow inside the egg because there is a store of food there. It is protected until it is ready to hatch.

With some animals, the babies grow from an egg inside the female. This happened to you.

Below are pictures of animals. Put a circle round those animals where the egg stays inside the body.

Put a square round the animals where the eggs are laid.

Draw a picture of the baby of each of these animals.

What size are the eggs? See if you can find out.

Draw a 'line-up' starting with the smallest egg at one end and with the largest at the other. Label each egg, saying which animal it belongs to.

How long does it take for the baby to be born?

67 Link the baby with its carer

℗ Purpose

To increase awareness of methods of birth.
To develop vocabulary of animals and their young.
To encourage library retrieval skills.

＞ Suggested age range

All ages.

∅ Materials needed

Photocopies of picture on p.175.

◕ Approximate timing

Variable.

▶ What else it relates to

Happy birthways!
Know-how
Stages of pregnancy

●● Numbers involved

Whole class, or small groups.

What to do

The teacher distributes the pictures and arranges children into groups (for ideas to do this, see Chapter 3).

The teacher encourages the children to list all of the animals that they can see. (With younger children this could be done as a class activity.)

The children can find out the names for each animal's babies, e.g. swan: cygnet.

Individually, children can colour in each animal and its young in the same colour.

Referring to their list of animals, the children can group them according to the way that the young are born, e.g. from an egg inside the female.

Older children can research gestation periods of the different animals and can produce a bar chart for classroom display.

Variations

A pile of blank cards (playing card size) is made available.

The children are invited to draw one picture on each card of an animal and its young. They may also make a word card to relate to that animal. Another card may indicate the gestation period. A further card might say, for example, 'Inside the body' or 'Outside the body', referring to the method of birth.

All of the cards are then available for class use at any time to play games such as *Happy Families* or even *Sibling Snap*!

It is more than likely that the children will suggest various follow-up activities on this theme.

67 Link the baby with its carer

68 Stages of pregnancy

Ⓟ **Purpose**

To develop an understanding of the stages of pregnancy.
To develop an awareness of sequencing.

> **Suggested age range**

All ages.

✎ **Materials needed**

Photocopy of p.177, cut up for each group.

◕ **Approximate timing**

Variable according to age.

▶ **What else it relates to**

Happy birthways!
Link the baby with its carer
Know-how

👥 **Numbers involved**

Small groups, or whole class.

What to do

Younger children, in groups of three or four, can put the pictures in the right sequence. The teacher then inputs information, choosing from the information boxes underneath the female images.

With older children, the teacher can distribute the images along with the separate information boxes. In groups, the children can sequence the pictures and then attempt to match the information to the images.

This activity can be done as an introduction to the topic of pregnancy. Here the teacher will have the opportunity to build on the children's ideas and questions.

Alternatively, it can be used as a reinforcement activity after children have received information from either the teacher or a video (see Resource list in Chapter 7).

68 Stages of pregnancy

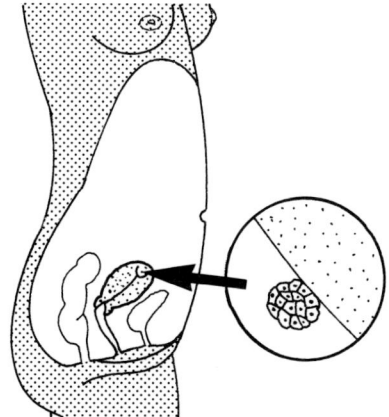

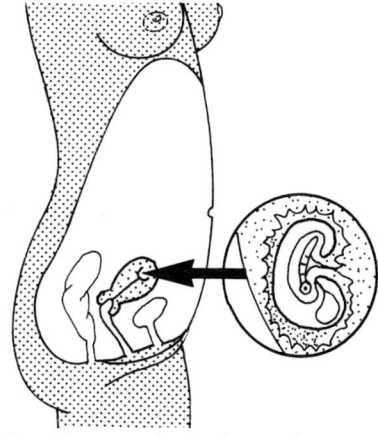

3 weeks

The fertilised egg is too small to be seen without a microscope, but the egg cells are multiplying rapidly.

6 weeks

The fertilised egg has now formed an embryo which looks like a tadpole.

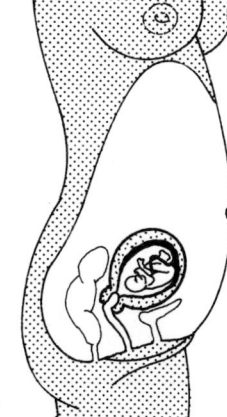

8 weeks

The embryo has developed arms and legs with perfectly shaped fingers and toes. It is now called a foetus.

12 weeks

The foetus is 3 inches long. It can kick its legs, close its fingers, turn its head and close its mouth. Most of its internal organs work.

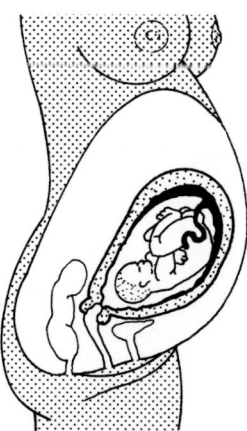

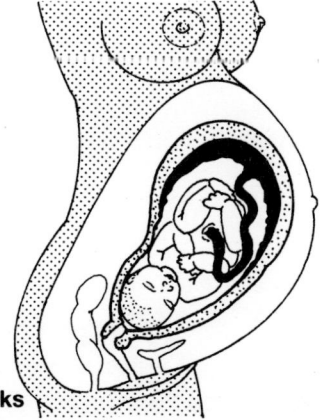

24 weeks

The baby has grown so much that people can see the mother is pregnant. Its heart can be heard through a stethoscope. The mother can feel the baby moving.

30 weeks

The baby is nearly ready to be born. The muscles inside the mother's womb push the baby out through the vagina. Most babies are born head first.

69 Know-how

Ⓟ Purpose

To offer a model of the type of worksheet that teachers can 'tailor make' for their children.

To identify what children have understood.

To offer an example of a worksheet that the children can design for others.

＞ Suggested age range

Upper Juniors.

⫽ Materials needed

Photocopies of worksheet on p.179, pens or pencils.

◕ Approximate timing

10–15 minutes.

▶ What else it relates to

Checking out the facts
Happy birthways!
Link the baby with its carer
Stages of pregnancy

👥 Numbers involved

Individuals.

What to do

The teacher makes the worksheet available for individuals.

The teacher may wish to encourage children to devise their own 'cloze procedure' sheet.

69 Know-how

Fill in the gaps. Choose the correct words from the box.

A baby begins as a tiny egg. Eggs are stored in a woman's body. The place where they

are stored is the _____. There are two _____. About

every _____ days, the ovaries release an _____ which

travels down _____ to the place where it can grow into a baby, which

is called the _____. The egg cannot grow into a baby until it is

_____ by _____, which comes from a man's

_____. The sperm is produced in the man's _____

which hang down behind the man's penis.

---

ovaries	egg	womb
	fertilised	28
tubes	sperm	penis
	testicles	ovary

Look at the words above. List the words which belong to a woman and the words
which belong to a man, and any which belong to both.

_____

☐ Birth control

You may have added to our brainstorm on why people have sex (see p.152). Many people have sex for reasons other than procreation. Becoming pregnant can be avoided. A list of current birth control methods is on pp. 181–184.

Note that this whole area is extremely value-laden and is dependent upon one's cultural/religious beliefs on the subject, or lack of them.

'If people have sex, and this can make babies happen, why do they not have lots and lots of children?'

We suggest that the theme of contraception is handled initially by looking at analogies within the children's experiences. As our example, we use the theme of barriers (see p.185).

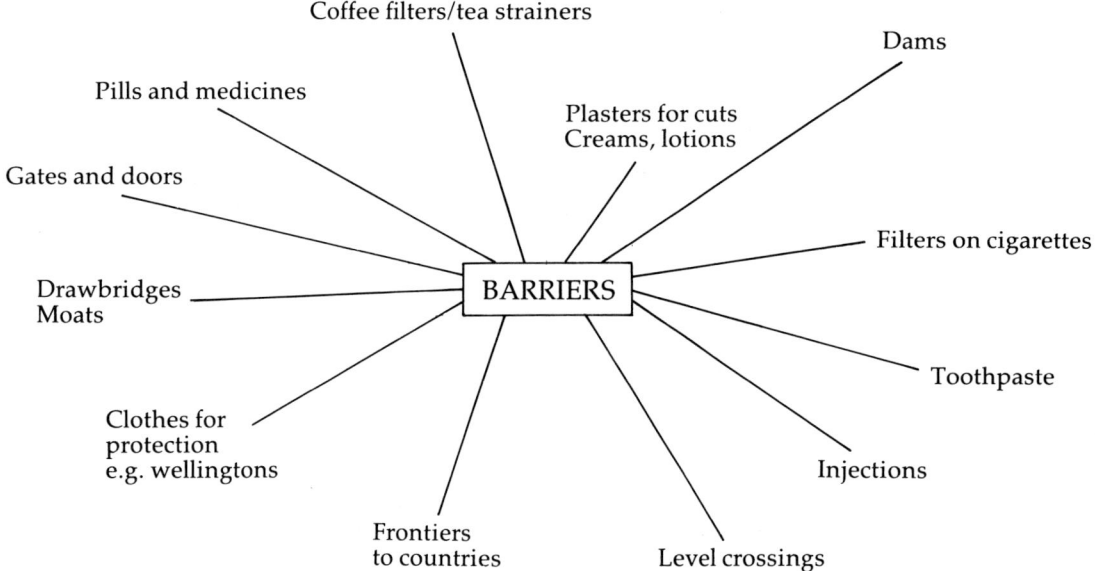

Abortion and miscarriage

Abortion should not be seen as a method of birth control, although it does stop unwanted pregnancies. The lining and contents of the womb are removed, either by gentle suction or by scraping with a surgical instrument. If the pregnancy is further advanced, labour can be induced and the foetus is expelled before it is able to survive.

Miscarriage occurs when, for one reason or another, the body rejects the foetus, which is spontaneously expelled.

You will be aware that these experiences can be extremely traumatic and upsetting, both for the person concerned and for those around them. There may be children in your class who have knowledge of such situations.

Birth control methods

Vasectomy

A minor operation for a man, in which the tubes which carry the sperm to the penis are cut and tied.

For

Does not affect your sex life. Relieves couple of necessity for other forms of contraception.

Against

Not generally reversible, so should be done only when the man is absolutely sure that he does not want any more children.

Sterilisation

A minor operation for a woman, in which the tubes carrying the egg to the womb are cut and blocked.

For

Relatively simple operation (though not without risks) which takes away the necessity for using contraception.

Against

Not as simple as vasectomy. Generally not reversible, so not recommended unless the woman has had all the children that she may want.

Pill

A chemical, taken in the form of a daily pill, which prevents the woman's body from releasing a new egg each month, so that pregnancy cannot occur.

For

Very effective.

Against

Some women have side effects.

— Cap

Also called the Diaphragm. A thin rubber dome, with a rigid edge, which the woman fits over her cervix before intercourse. It prevents sperm from getting into the womb. Should be used with a sperm-killing cream or foam to be really effective.

For

Can be used again and again. May give protection against cancer of the cervix.

Against

In the first instance needs to be properly fitted by a doctor.

— I.U.D. (Inter Uterine Device)

A small (2.5–4 cm long) plastic and copper device, which is inserted by a doctor into the woman's womb. It works by preventing any fertilised egg from settling there.

For

Can be left in place for several years.

Against

Not a first choice method for young women. In some women it can cause excessively heavy periods, pain or cramps.

— Condom

Sometimes called a 'rubber' or 'johnny'. A thin rubber tube which unrolls to fit over the erect penis. It has a teat at the end to catch the semen after ejaculation.

For

Easy to obtain (from chemists or Family Planning Clinics) and easy to use. Can protect against STDs, including HIV infection, and may protect women against cancer of the cervix.

Against

Important to put one on before penetration. Must be taken off carefully. Needs gentle handling, otherwise can split if roughly treated.

— Sponge

A new method involving a soft circular sponge made of polyurethane foam, which is put in the woman's vagina before she has intercourse. It contains enough spermicide to kill any sperm for up to 24 hours.

For

Easy to obtain from chemists and easy to use.

Against

Expensive, especially as it is used once only then thrown away. Not as effective as some other methods.

— Natural Methods

Also called the Rhythm Method. The couple need to work out when the woman's most fertile days are each month, so that intercourse may be avoided during that time.

For

Needs the co-operation and commitment of both partners.

Against

Not very effective, especially where the woman's cycle is not regular. Not suitable for people in casual relationships.

— Spermicides

Chemicals (usually sold in cream, foam, jelly or pessary form) which kill sperm when inserted in the woman's vagina. Not very effective when used on their own. Usually used with another method, e.g. condom or cap.

— Celibacy

Sometimes people make a choice not to be involved in sexual relationships with others, either for a short time or sometimes permanently.

___ Withdrawal _____

When the man withdraws his erect penis from the woman's vagina, just before he ejaculates, or climaxes. Sometimes called 'pulling out'. *Not* an effective method of contraception, since there may be sperm present in the fluid at the tip of the penis before the man comes.

___ 'Morning-after' (or post-coital), pill _____

Contraceptive pill which can be taken within 72 hours of an act of unprotected intercourse to prevent implantation of the fertilised ovum. Only available on prescription from a doctor or family planning clinic.

For

Useful for emergencies if conception is likely to have taken place.

Against

Not recommended as a regular form of contraception.

70 Barriers

℗ **Purpose**

To enable the children to understand the concept of contraception.

> **Suggested age range**

Upper Juniors.

✎ **Materials needed**

Large sheets of paper, felt-tipped pens.

◕ **Approximate timing**

30 minutes.

▶ **What else it relates to**

Baby talk

👤👤 **Numbers involved**

Whole class divided into groups of three or four.

What to do

The teacher begins the lesson by demonstrating what a flow-chart looks like. The example on p.180 is concerned with barriers but the teacher should choose a different subject for the initial work.

The children will be able to help to produce the flow-chart by offering ideas, which are recorded by the teacher. Once the children have understood the process, they are divided into small groups and asked to produce their own flow-chart on the subject of barriers.

When they have completed this, debrief questions will include:

'Did each group think of the same barriers?'
'Do all barriers work as well as each other?'
'Why does their effectiveness vary?'

The teacher may then proceed to introduce the topic of contraception.

71 Baby talk

(P) **Purpose**

To explore reasons for choosing to have children or not.
To introduce the idea that people have a choice.

> **Suggested age range**

Top Juniors.

Materials needed

Large sheets of paper, felt-tipped pens.

Approximate timing

30 minutes.

▶ **What else it relates to**

Barriers

Numbers involved

Whole class divided into four groups.

_____ **What to do** _____

The teacher divides the class into four groups.

Two groups discuss and list all the reasons that they can think of for people wanting to have babies. The other groups discuss and list all the reasons why people choose not to have children.

The groups who were doing the same task then share their work and ideas.

Then the teacher asks the two groups who were doing different tasks to share their work. A whole class discussion can take place.

☐ STDs and AIDS

Should we be teaching about STDs and AIDS in the primary school classroom?

This will depend upon the policy/curricular statement that your school has about sex education. However, the children are likely to ask questions and it is a matter for individual teachers to determine what might be appropriate responses. As it is an extremely sensitive and contentious area, it is important that teachers meet to discuss their feelings and views about it.

In some areas, courses have been arranged. Entitled 'Dealing with controversial issues in the classroom', these have covered issues such as contraception, abortion, STDs and AIDS, and have been extremely well received.

Alternatively, if your school staff would like to spend time looking at some of these issues, the LEA's Adviser or Advisory Teacher for PSE (Personal and Social Education) or Health Education may be able to help. Health Education/Promotion Units of the local Health Authority could also be approached, since most of them are involved in developing work with schools.

We feel very strongly that teachers should focus on positive aspects of sex and personal relationships. Teaching about diseases and viruses can present a very bleak picture to the primary school child, so the teacher needs to think very carefully about when and how to introduce these areas.

HIV and AIDS: points to bear in mind

1 The transmission of HIV has to do with risky behaviour, and not with particular so-called 'high risk groups'. The teacher may become aware of prejudice in the classroom and this needs to be challenged and corrected. Homophobic and racist attitudes are, unfortunately, widespread. Primary schools are not immune to their pervasive influence.

The AIDS epidemic is not a 'gay plague'. In many parts of the world it manifests itself largely in the heterosexual population. Medical experts are predicting that, in the next 10–20 years, there will be a steady increase of AIDS amongst heterosexuals. The children in your class will be sexually active then.

2 HIV (Human Immuno-deficiency Virus) is often thought to be a virus unlike any other. It must be stressed that, whilst HIV does have distinct differences from other viruses, it also shares many of their characteristics.

It cannot be said too often that it is very difficult for the virus to be passed from one person to another. It cannot be 'caught'. In many

187

ways HIV is weaker than most viruses. It cannot live outside the body for very long. It enters the bloodstream either through the exchange of bodily fluids (semen, vaginal fluid) during sex or through the use of shared drug-injecting equipment.

3   HIV is different from AIDS. When someone is HIV Antibody Positive, it means that s/he has antibodies to HIV. S/he may well be perfectly healthy and symptom free. If s/he goes on to develop AIDS (Acquired Immuno-Deficiency Syndrome), it is not one disease but a condition in which opportunistic infections, such as pneumonia, can affect the person whose immune system is being attacked and weakened. It is by no means certain that all people who are HIV Antibody Positive will go on to develop AIDS. 'Living with HIV and AIDS' is a positive concept, which ought to be emphasised, unlike the very negative 'AIDS = Death' view which is propagated by the tabloid press and others.

4   Children need to understand that everyday contact with others will not lead to transmission of the virus. They can hug and kiss people who have the virus, share food, swim together, and generally enjoy their company.

5   HIV/AIDS is sometimes seen as a punishment for 'wrong' behaviour. This is not the case. Such 'non-wrongdoers' as people with haemophilia became HIV+ before blood was screened in this country and elsewhere. In this connection, the media have made same-sex relationships appear 'wrong' and have dubbed AIDS as the 'gay plague', but it is interesting to note that the disease is practically unknown amongst the lesbian community. Teachers must ensure that erroneous or ignorant statements are challenged and corrected.

Similarly, children ought to know that the virus can be passed on to the unborn child in the womb. There are children who are HIV+ because their mothers have passed the virus on to them. Other children and young people became antibody positive through receiving contaminated blood before all blood products were heat-treated in some countries to prevent this from happening.

In the years to come there will be more HIV+ children coming through the school system. Teachers need to be knowledgeable so that they are prepared to deal with this. There has been some debate as to who should be informed about a child in school who is HIV+. We think that there is nothing to be gained by its being common knowledge in a school. We have only to look at the way in which some HIV+ children were excluded from school in the USA to realise that the underlying philosophy should be: 'Who needs to know?'

Most local education authorities have issued guidelines to schools about HIV and AIDS, which should include information about the control of infection. The ILEA Circular of April 1987, *Guidance to Staff about the AIDS Virus*, stated: 'Normal first aid, hygiene and

I HAVE AiDS
PLease hug me

I can't make you sick

cleaning procedures should be followed for any bleeding injuries that may occur in schools.' Hopefully all LEAs are updating their advice to schools about hygiene measures and calling the virus HIV, not the AIDS virus.

6   In answering questions about how and where AIDS started, the teacher must counteract any homophobic and racist conjectures. Apart from this, it is not useful to dwell on the origins of the condition, especially with young children, as it can deflect from other more important considerations.

7   The question of condoms might well come up. The teacher must emphasise that the use of condoms is a responsible act if people choose to have penetrative sex with a partner.

Teaching about diseases and viruses

One way in which HIV, AIDS and STDs might be tackled in the primary school is in the context of work about illness and disease. (It is vital that this sort of work is *not* done in isolation.)

Children should be aware that diseases can be spread in different ways before looking at specific cases, such as AIDS or STDs.

They will need to have done work on **Non-infectious diseases**, such as heart disease, arthritis, diabetes, cancer. They must also have done some work on **infectious diseases**, which involves an understanding that germs can enter the body and bring about changes within it. Examples might be colds, 'flu or measles. However, we feel that learning about HIV and AIDS might be more positively done within the context of 'keeping ourselves safe'.

During their studies, children should have come to realise that not all bacteria are harmful. Indeed, some are used in the processes of food making, e.g. yoghurt, cheese, beer.

☐ Continuum activities

It is difficult to ascertain the experiences and knowledge that the children have regarding many of the more explicit areas of sexual activity.

In helping children to understand, we have found it useful to use the activities on pp. 191–197. They encourage children to express ideas and to identify issues.

For example, the Whole class continuum A can be used prior to a factual input, and Small group continuum A afterwards.

These activities will show up areas where children have misconceptions. It is vital that these misconceptions are addressed by the teacher.

72 Whole class continuum A: facts

Ⓟ Purpose

To encourage children to explore areas of knowledge.

> Suggested age range

Upper Juniors.

✏ Materials needed

Large space, e.g. a hall. Two large sheets of paper (one entitled True, the other False).

List of statements to be read out which relate to a forthcoming knowledge input by the teacher. (See sample statements on pp. 195–197).

◑ Approximate timing

20 minutes.

▶ Numbers involved

Whole class.

👥 What else it relates to

Any area where knowledge needs to be explored.

What to do

The teacher displays the sheet of paper entitled True at one end of the room, and the sheet entitled False at the other end of the room, and indicates these to the children. The teacher also points out an imaginary line joining one to the other.

The teacher then reads out a statement which relates to a forthcoming subject to be covered. The children are asked to stand at some point on the line, according to whether they think the statement is true or false. It is helpful if the teacher points out that they do not have to go to one extremity or the other. They can be somewhere in the middle. Also, it is important that the teacher explains that the children's uncertainty or lack of knowledge will be addressed immediately following the activity.

When the children are standing on the imaginary line, they can be encouraged to talk to each other about why they are standing where they are. The teacher can ask different children to explain why they are standing at that particular place.

In our experience, when children first participate in this activity, some tend to follow others, rather than think for themselves. We have found this a useful teaching point in itself.

73 Small group continuum A: facts

(P) **Purpose**

To encourage children to explore areas of knowledge.

> **Suggested age range**

Upper Juniors.

Materials needed

For each group, large sheets of paper, felt-tipped pens, small cards with facts written on them, Blu-tak.

Approximate timing

30 minutes.

▶ **What else it relates to**

Any area where knowledge needs to be explored.

Numbers involved

Whole class divided into small groups.

What to do

The teacher divides the class into groups of three or four and distributes sets of cards and one large sheet of paper to each group.

The children draw a horizontal line on the paper and write 'True' at one end and 'False' at the other. The cards are placed face down in the middle of each group.

The teacher should explain that each child will take it in turn to take a card and place it along the continuum. It is important to emphasise that the card may be placed anywhere along the continuum, and not necessarily at one end or the other. The other children in the group can help to inform the child with the card about where to place it. Once the group has decided where the card should go, the children use Blu-tak to attach it to the paper.

This activity will inform the teacher of any misunderstandings the children may have.

74 Whole class continuum B: feelings

(P) Purpose

To encourage children to explore issues together.

> Suggested age range

Upper Juniors.

Materials needed

Large space, e.g. a hall. Two large sheets of paper (one entitled True, the other False).

List of statements to be read out which relate to a forthcoming knowledge input by the teacher. (See sample statements on pp. 195–197).

Approximate timing

20 minutes.

What else it relates to

Any area where attitudes need to be explored.

Numbers involved

Whole class.

What to do

The teacher displays the sheet of paper entitled Agree at one end of the room, and the sheet of paper entitled Disagree at the other end of the room, and indicates these to the children. The teacher also points out an imaginary line joining one to the other.

The teacher then reads out a statement which relates to issues. The children are asked to stand at some point on the line, according to whether they agree with the statement or not. It is helpful if the teacher points out that they do not have to go to one extremity or the other. They can be somewhere in the middle.

When the children are standing on the imaginary line, they can be encouraged to talk to each other about why they are standing where they are. The teacher can ask different children to explain why they are standing at that particular place.

In our experience, when children first participate in this activity, some tend to follow others, rather than think for themselves. We have found this a useful teaching point in itself.

75 Small group continuum B: feelings

Ⓟ **Purpose**

To encourage children to explore issues and attitudes.

> **Suggested age range**

Upper Juniors.

Materials needed

For each group, large sheets of paper, felt-tipped pens, small cards with issues written on them, Blu-tak.

Approximate timing

30 minutes.

▶ **What else it relates to**

Any area where attitudes need to be explored.

Numbers involved

Whole class divided into small groups.

What to do

The teacher divides the class into groups of three or four and distributes sets of cards and one large sheet of paper to each group.

The children draw a horizontal line on the paper and write 'Agree' at one end and 'Disagree' at the other. The cards are placed face down in the middle of each group.

The teacher should explain that each child will take it in turn to take a card and place it along the continuum. It is important to emphasise that the card may be placed anywhere along the continuum, and not necessarily at one end or the other. The other children in the group can help to inform the child with the card about where to place it. Once the group has decided where the card should go, the children use Blu-tak to attach it to the paper.

In this way, the teacher has a record of the attitudes of the children towards certain issues.

76 Continuum activities: suggested statements

These statements concern sexual activity. You may wish to modify or change them.

_____

Masturbation can be bad for you.

_____

People always have sex in bed.

_____

You have to be 16 years old to have sex.

_____

Men are more interested in sexual activity than women are.

_____

For sexual activity, the man has to lie on top of the woman.

_____

There is nothing wrong with feeling attracted to someone of the same sex.

_____

People lose interest in sex when they get old.

_____

You have to be married to have sex.

_____

Lots of people say that they have had sex when they have not.

_____

The amount of fluid produced during sexual activity is very little.

_____

Some people are virgins all their lives.

_____

76 Continuum activities: suggested statements

These statements relate to gender issues. You may wish to modify or change them.

_____

It is wrong for little boys to play with dolls.

_____

It is natural for women to be more caring than men.

_____

Women are braver than men.

_____

Men should take an equal share of the housework.

_____

It is okay for boys to cry.

_____

Men should give up their seats for women on buses.

_____

It is okay for a girl to be a tomboy.

_____

It is okay for a boy to play with girls all the time.

_____

It is not okay for a girl to ask a boy out.

_____

Eleven-year old girls are always more grown up than boys of the same age.

_____

76 Continuum activities: suggested statements

These statements are to encourage discussion about other issues concerned with sex. You may wish to modify or change them. (See also the *Aide-mémoire* section, pp. 202–204.)

Women should be able to choose whether to have babies or not.

Hormones can cause mood changes before and during a woman's period.

It is embarrassing for a girl to carry a condom.

Contraception is the responsibility of both partners who have decided to have sex.

You cannot become HIV+ by kissing an infected person.

One in every ten people is sexually attracted to someone of the same sex.

There are times in people's lives when they may choose not to have sex with others.

People who are physically disabled often enjoy an active sex life.

Most children of ten think that sex is an odd thing for people to want to do.

Nobody should be allowed to touch my body if I feel uneasy about it.

77 Diamond fours/nines

Ⓟ Purpose

To enable the children to consider their personal view about any issue.

To encourage them to share these views and to argue their importance.

> Suggested age range

Juniors. Diamond fours is a simpler version, so would be more appropriate for younger children.

✐ Materials needed

For each child, an envelope containing four/nine pieces of paper each with a statement written on it. Examples of the types of statements you might wish to use can be found on pp. 200–201.

◔ Approximate timing

30 minutes.

▶ What else it relates to

Any area where issues are being discussed.

▲▲ Numbers involved

Whole class, individually, then in pairs. It is possible to continue in fours.

_____ What to do _____

Before the lesson, the teacher decides which statements should be written on each piece of paper. (The suggested statements are only examples. This activity is very versatile.)

The teacher distributes the envelopes with the pieces of paper inside. For Diamond fours, the teacher asks the children to rank the statements, putting what they feel is the most important statement at the top, and the least important at the bottom. In between they will place the other two statements, making a diamond as follows:

$$
\begin{array}{lll}
\text{X} & = & \text{Most important statement} \\
\text{X X} & = & \text{Next most important statements} \\
\text{X} & = & \text{Least important statement}
\end{array}
$$

For Diamond nines, the process is slightly different. Again they will place the most important statement at the top and the least important at the bottom. In between, however, they have to rank the remaining statements in order of importance to make a larger diamond as follows:

X	=	Most important statement
X X	=	Next two most important statements
X X X	=	Next three most important statements
X X	=	Next two most important statements
X	=	Least important statement

For the children to understand this, the teacher needs to demonstrate the process carefully.

Once the children have formed their diamond individually, they work in pairs to share their ideas. Because this activity is to encourage children to analyse their attitudes, it may be a good idea for them to try to convince their partner about their diamond shape, explaining the reasons why they have done it in the way that they have. Obviously each partner is trying to convince the other. In this way, they may have to reach a compromise.

Debrief questions will include:

'Did you agree about the most important? If not, why not?'
'Which statements caused the most discussion for you?'
'Did your partner manage to change your mind?'
'What have you learned about your partner by doing this?'
'What have you learned about yourself?'

78 Diamond fours/nines: suggested statements

Most of these statements could be used either for the continuum activities or for Diamond fours or Diamond nines. You may wish to modify or change them.

A good friend is . . .

_____

Someone who will stick up for me.

_____

Someone who will tell me the truth.

_____

Someone who makes me laugh.

_____

Someone who will listen to what I am saying.

_____

Someone who will share their belongings with me.

_____

Someone who has lots of good ideas.

_____

Someone who wears fashionable clothes.

_____

Someone who is liked by my family.

_____

Someone who is the same age as me.

_____

78 Diamond fours/nines: suggested statements

I can keep myself safe by . . .

_____

Talking to others.

_____

Saying no.

_____

Never going to dangerous places.

_____

Not talking to strangers.

_____

Always being home on time.

_____

Telling others where I am going.

_____

Never keeping secrets.

_____

Not being afraid to shout if necessary.

_____

Fighting back.

_____

79 *Aide-mémoire*

Throughout this book, there are sections which provide information for the teacher. This is to help with the formulation of the sex education programme which is offered to primary school children. There are other areas which you may wish to consider. Children will be aware of many of them. Have you remembered to include the following, for example?

— *Crushes*

These are very common. Crushes may relate to people whom children actually know or people such as pop stars. It is quite common to have a crush on someone of the same sex.

— *Erections*

Unwanted erections can be very embarrassing and can happen at any time, even though boys may not be thinking about sex. As with many aspects of sex education, young people need to be reassured that this is perfectly normal. A common worry about erections is that semen and urine may be released at the same time. This is biologically impossible.

— *Fantasies*

Most children play fantasy games. As they grow older many young people have sexual fantasies. Boys and girls may masturbate while fantasising. This is normal behaviour. Teachers may wish to encourage children to learn about masturbation and to dispel myths such as 'masturbation can make you go blind'. One way of tackling the subject is through a worksheet (see p.169). Worksheets of this nature are merely a guide, and teachers may wish to adapt such an approach to meet the needs of their children.

— *Foreplay*

This is a word usually used to describe sexual activity prior to penetration. It may involve kissing, licking and touching parts of the body to sexually arouse the partner. Various parts of the body are especially sensitive to touch. Penetration is only one form of sexual expression: what some people describe as foreplay is a complete sexual act for others.

— *Incest*

Strictly speaking, this is sexual intercourse between people who are closely related to each other. It is taboo, culturally and legally, in most societies. Incest is closely connected to the sexual abuse of children, since research shows that girls are more often the victims of sexual abuse than boys, and that the offender is often the girl's father or step-father.

Moods

During puberty, young people can feel very moody. The hormones in the body are changing and this is one of the factors. It is important to acknowledge that these moods may happen.

Petting

This is a general term used to describe kissing, cuddling and touching each other's bodies. People also talk about heavy petting, which might include kissing by placing the tongue in the other person's mouth, and the touching of sexual organs. Petting is often the first experience that young people have of expressing sexual feelings for each other.

Rape

Most children will have heard of this word. While it is true that rape means forcing somebody to have sex against their will, it must be stressed that rape is an act of violence, and is about power. It is not a sexual act which gives pleasure to both parties.

Sexuality

This is difficult to define. It concerns how people identify with and adopt a specific gender role, and their feelings about this. It also relates to the biological condition of being female or male. From birth, boys learn to be boys, and girls to be girls.

Size

Each person's body is individual to that person. People do worry about size and shape. For example, in females the size of the breasts is often a concern, and males may worry about the size of the penis, and whether they have a foreskin or not. All of these variations in size and appearance are normal, and make no difference when it comes to enjoying sexual activity.

Sexually Transmitted Diseases (STDS)

A whole range of infections from syphilis and gonorrhoea (still often referred to by the old term venereal diseases), HIV and AIDS through to others which are more accurately described as infections of the genital or urinary tract (genito-urinary) and are not sexually transmitted. They include non-specific urethritis (NSU), trichomoniases, genital herpes, thrush, cystitis and pelvic inflammatory disease (PID).

Voice changes

As children grow, the larynx grows bigger. Males have bigger voice boxes and therefore deeper voices. During puberty, the muscles of the larynx sometimes go out of control for a few seconds. This can result in sudden squeaky sounds, which some boys find embarrassing.

Wet dreams

These happen when there has been an accumulation of semen. During sleep, the semen is released. This may occur in the course of dreams that involve sexual fantasies. Wet dreams are common and harmless.

·7·
You'll get by with a little help from...

You will realise that this book is based on ways of working which are:

Active

Based on empowerment of people

Concerned with values

Developmental (building on earlier experiences)

Experimental (encouraging the learning to come from children's first-hand knowledge)

Friendly, (the activities are designed to be non-threatening)

Group-oriented

Holistic (concerned with the development of the whole child)

Innovative

Judgement-free

Known to work

The authors are experienced facilitators in the area of personal, social and health education. They are able to offer further training to develop ideas within this sphere.

☐ Looking at resources

It is unfortunate that there are not many sex education resources for the primary school child. We feel that it is important that you should have a look at the materials that are suggested later in this section and judge whether they are suitable for your age range.

It may be helpful to try out the workshop to generate criteria for selection of resources (see pp. 208–209).

Do remember that resources can date quickly.

Do consider
- multi-cultural needs.
- different religious beliefs.
- the relevance of the resource to the child, in terms of class, urban/rural setting.
- the degree of familiarity for the child. Are the illustrations in the resource what the child normally sees?
- that you may give hidden messages when using the resource: teachers must feel comfortable with the resource that they are using.
- all types of stereotyping, e.g. disability, race.

Do remember
- to look at how men and women are portrayed in the resource.
- to check if the resource is compatible with the agreed style of sex education of your school.
- to check if the resource is attractive.
- to assess if the resource respects the child and is not patronising.

80 Resources workshop

This workshop is adaptable for use with teachers, parents and governors.

Purpose

To share participants' experiences of various resources, and to use these to identify what makes a good resource.

To identify criteria for choosing resources for sex education.

To use these criteria to review actual resources.

To generate a list of resources which the school could use.

Introduction

This is to welcome the participants and to outline the session, which will be active and participatory.

Ice-breaker

This is to help participants to feel comfortable. You may wish to choose an idea from this book. A particularly useful one is on p. 212.

Drawing on participants' experiences

In groups of three or four, ask participants to think of a resource which they found useful/fun and which has worked well with children. What did they like about it? Why was it useful? What made it work?

This is to help the group to focus on successful resources which they have used. They may wish to list their ideas.

Feedback

This enables participants to share any thoughts from the previous activity.

Brainstorm

The question is: 'What are the components of a good sex education resource?'

Once the list has been generated, participants can work in smaller groups to consider the following questions.

Reflection time

'Could these be the criteria for judging a resource for sex education and personal relationships?'

'What additions or subtractions would you make?'

Feedback

This will give an opportunity for the whole group to consider additions and subtractions to the original list and to firm it up.

Participants can be asked to work in pairs to review resources.

Using a checklist

A photocopy of the checklist on pp. 210–211 may be helpful.

In pairs, the participants evaluate their chosen resource, with reference to both the checklist and the brainstorm which has been generated and amended by the group.

Feedback

Sharing ideas about the resource.

Closing activity

After collection of written reviews, a closing activity is a good idea. See Chapter 3 for suggestions.

80 Resource checklist

TITLE: ....

AUTHOR(S): ....

PUBLISHER: ....

ISBN: ....

THIS RESOURCE SEEMS TO BE AIMED AT: ....

....

The main topics that it covers are: ....

....

....

The aim of the resource seems to be: ....

....

....

The illustrations used are appropriate/inappropriate because: ....

....

....

The size of print is appropriate/inappropriate because: ....

....

....

The language used is appropriate/inappropriate because: ....

....

....

80 Resource checklist

The social settings are appropriate/inappropriate because: ....

....

....

The following groups are positively/negatively represented: ....

....

....

The settings are appropriate/inappropriate to the children's experiences in the

following ways: ....

....

....

We would use the resource in the following way: ....

....

....

The sample checklist is designed for printed resources.
Statements useful for other kinds of resource might include:
- The pace of the video is appropriate/inappropriate because:
- The tones of voice used are appropriate/inappropriate because:
- The rules of the game are suitable/unsuitable because:
- The quality of reproduction is . . .
- The teacher's notes are . . .

80 Resources workshop: ice-breaker

Here is a list of famous pairs:

Romeo and Juliet
Sherlock Holmes and Dr Watson
Elizabeth Taylor and Richard Burton
Laurence Olivier and Joan Plowright
Nelson and Winnie Mandela
Butch Cassidy and the Sundance Kid
Bette Davis and Joan Crawford

You may want to make up your own.

Each participant has a piece of paper pinned to her/his back, on which you have written the name of one of the people from the list.

The participants have to identify the name of the person by asking questions of each other. Only 'Yes/No' answers are allowed.

Participants can then find their famous partner.

This activity should be done standing up and milling around.

☐ Resources

― Introduction ―

The resources mentioned in this section are only a proportion of those available. Primary schools may already have their own collections, built up over time, but other places you will find useful are:

- Teacher's centres, which generally have resource collections.
- Local libraries.
- Health Education/Promotion Units, which are part of district Health Authorities. They are usually listed as such in the phone book, but may also be contacted through the Liaison Section of the Health Education Authority, or through your local Community Health Council.

Many resources are listed in the following free publications:

- *Teaching Materials for Children 5–8* (a resource list with relevance to Health Education)
- *Books for Children 5–8* (annotated bibliography with relevance to Health Education)

Both lists are also available for the 9–13 age group and may be obtained from the Information Centre, Health Education Authority, Hamilton House, Mabledon Place, London WC1H 9TX.

Materials and resources are coded as follows:

TR	=	Teacher Resource
PR	=	Pupil Resource
B	=	Book
TP	=	Teaching Pack
TV	=	Off-air Schools TV Programme
V	=	Video
G	=	Games
S	=	This resource is intended for the secondary age range, but we feel that it can be adapted for use in the primary school.
SL	=	Slides
CH	=	Chart

___ 1 Everything you ever wanted to know about sex education . . . _____

B, TR   *Education in Sex and Personal Relationships*, Isobel Allen, Policy Studies Institute, 1987.

B, TR   *Sex Education: Some Guidelines for Teachers*, Dilys Went, Bell & Hyman, Modern Teaching Series, 1985.

B, TR   *School Sex Education: Why, What and How?*, Doreen Massey, FPA Education Unit, 1988.

V, TR   *It's Sex Next Week* (1985), Central Independent Television Video Resources Unit, Central House, Broad Street, Birmingham B1 2JP.

TV, PR   *Sex Education* (1990), three programmes: 'Growing', 'Someone New', 'Life Begins'. Check BBC Catalogue for transmission details. Also available for sale from BBC TV Enterprises Ltd, Education and Training Sales, Woodlands, 80 Wood Lane, London W12 0TT.

TP, TR   *Sex Education Fact Pack* (1988), FPA Education Unit, 27–35 Mortimer Street, London W1N 7RJ.

B, TR   *Sex Education At School*, Circular No. 11/87, Dept of Education and Science, 1987. DES Publications Despatch Centre, Canons Park, Honeypot Lane, Stanmore, Middlesex HA7 1AZ.

B, TR   *Sexwise* (ILEA)

B, TR   *Sexual Issues, the Law and the Teacher's Responsibility* (1987), Assistant Masters and Mistresses Association, 7 Northumberland Street, London WC2N 5DA.

B, TR, S   *The Ostrich Position: Sex, Schooling and Mystification*, Carol Lee, Unwin Hyman, 1986.

B, TR   *Children's Sexual Thinking*, R. and J. Goldman, Routledge & Kegan Paul, 1983.

B, TR, S   *Taught Not Caught: Strategies for Sex Education*, The Clarity Collective (2nd ed.), LDA, 1988.

___ 3 Making it happen _____

B, TR   *Thinking About Personal and Social Education in the Primary School*, Peter Lang (ed.), Basil Blackwell, 1988.

B, TR   *Personal Values in Primary Education*, Norman Kirby, Harper & Row, 1981.

TP, TR, PR   *Health for Life, Parts 1 and 2*, HEA Primary School Project, Nelson, 1989.

TP, TR, PR   *All About Me* (5–8) and *Think Well* (9–13), Schools Council Health Education Project, Nelson, 1977.

TP, TR, PR   *Fit For Life*, J. McNaughton, HEA Health Education for Slow Learners Project, Macmillan, 1983.

TP, TR, PR   *My Body*, Health Education Council Project, Heinemann, 1983.

B, TR, PR   *Global Teacher, Global Learner*, G. Pike and D. Selby, Hodder & Stoughton, 1988.

B, TR, PR, S   *A Guide To Student Centred Learning*, D. Brandes and P. Ginnis, Basil Blackwell, 1986.

B, TR, PR, S   *Gamesters' Handbook*, D. Brandes and H. Phillips, Hutchinson, 1979.

B, TR, PR   *World Studies 8–13: A Teacher's Handbook*, S. Fisher and D.W. Hicks, Oliver & Boyd, 1985.

B, TR   *Health Education In Schools*, K. David and T. Williams (eds), Harper & Row, 1987.

B, TR   *Health Education: An Aspect of the Primary Curriculum*, ILEA Learning Resources, 1985.

4   Knowing me, knowing you

B, PR   *Let's Talk About Feeling Safe*, P. Sanders, Franklin Watts, 1987.

B, PR   *Let's Talk About Bullying*, A. Grunsell, Franklin Watts, 1989.

B, TR, PR   *Self-Esteem: A Classroom Affair*, M. & C. Borba, vol. 1 (1978), vol. 2 (1982), Minneapolis Winston Press.

B, TR, PR   *Let's Cooperate: Activities and Ideas for Teachers and Parents of Children Aged 3–11*, M. Masheder, Peace Education Project, 1986.

B, TR, S   *Just Like A Girl: How Girls Learn To Be Women*, Sue Sharpe, Penguin, 1981.

B, TR, PR   *Greater Expectations: A Source Book For Working With Girls and Young Women*, T. Szirom and S. Dyson, (2nd ed.), LDA, 1990.

B, TR, PR   *Coping With Conflict: A Resource Book For The Middle School Years*, F.M. Nicholas, LDA, 1987.

TP, PR   *Roles, Relationships, Responsibilities* (Pack of Trigger Drawings), Lambeth Health Education Project, ILEA Learning Resources, 1982.

B, TR   *Preventing Child Sexual Assault*, Michele Elliott, Bedford Square Press/NCVO, 1985.

B, TR   *Child Abuse: An Educational Perspective*, Peter Maher (ed.), Basil Blackwell, 1987.

B, TR   *Enhancing Self-Esteem in the Classroom*, D. Lawrence, Paul Chapman Publishing, 1988.

B, TR, PR   *Changing Images: Anti-Racist, Anti-Sexist Dawings*, N. Ninvalle, Sheba Feminist Publishers, 1984.

TV, PR   *Who – Me?* Check BBC Catalogue for transmission details.

TP, TR, PR   *Myself*, ACER, ILEA Learning Resources Branch, 1987.

___ 5 Nothing stays the same _____

B, PR   *Understanding the Facts Of Life*, S. Meredith and R. Gee, Usborne, 1985.

B, PR   *Have You Started Yet?*, R. Thomson, Piccolo, 1980.

B, PR   *The Body Book*, C. Rayner, Piccolo, 1979.

B, PR   *What's Happening to Me?*, P. Mayle, Macmillan, 1987.

SL, PR, TR   *It Happens To Us All: Puberty Kit*, 1983. Johnson and Johnson.

B, PR   *A Baby In The Family*, Althea, Dinosaur Publications, 1981.

B, PR   *Letters to Growing Pains*, Phillip Hodson, BBC Books, 1988.

B, PR   *See How You Grow*, P. Pearse, Macdonald, 1988.

B, PR, TR   *Growing Up*, Dr James Docherty, Modus Books/Royal Society of Medicine, 1986.

B, TR   *Our Bodies, Ourselves*, Boston Women's Health Book Collective, Penguin, 1989.

TP, TR   *Male and Female*, set of laminated A4 cards (1983), FPA Education Unit, 27–35 Mortimer Street, London W1N 7RJ.

CH, PR   *Growing Up*, set of four wall charts plus teacher's notes (1987), Pictorial Charts Educational Trust, 27 Kirchen Road, London W13 0UD.

CH, PR   *Rites of Passage: Initiation Rites*, set of four wall charts plus teacher's notes, (1987), Pictorial Charts Educational Trust, 27 Kirchen Road, London W13 0UD.

G, TR, PR   *Time of the Month* (1987), National Association of Youth Clubs, Keswick House, 30 Peacock Lane, Leicester LE1 5NY.

V, PR   *Growing Up: A Guide To Puberty* (1984), Bounty Vision Ltd, Bounty Services Ltd, Diss, Norfolk IP22 3HH.

V, PR   *Am I Normal?*, Boston Family Planning Project, 1979 (American film about adolescence in boys), Concord Ltd, 201 Felixstowe Road, Ipswich IP3 9BJ.

V, PR   *Having A Period*, Scottish Health Education Group, 1981, Boulton-Hawker Films Ltd, Hadleigh, Ipswich IP7 5BG.

— 6 What's love got to do with it? ———

B, PR *Let's Talk About AIDS*, P. Sanders and C. Farquhar, Franklin Watts, 1989.

B, PR *Where Did I Come From?*, P. Mayle, Macmillan, 1975.

V, PR *Where Did I Come From?* animated video based on the book, Virgin VVC 181.

SL, PR *The Baby*, colour filmstrip plus teacher's notes, Philip Green Educational, 1979.

B, PR *Inside Mum: Illustrated Account of Conception, Pregnancy and Childbirth*, Sylvia Caveney, Sidgwick & Jackson, 1986.

B, PR *The Story of Birth and Babies*, V.A. Prot and Dr P. Delorme, Moonlight Publishing, 1987.

TR *Positively Primary*, P. Sanders and C. Farquhar, 1990. AVERT, PO Box 91, Horsham, West Sussex RH13 7YR.